TAOISM

FOR BEGINNERS

A Guide to Balanced Living

TAOISM

FOR BEGINNERS

A Guide to Balanced Living

C. Alexander Simpkins and
Annellen Simpkins

TUTTLE Publishing
Tokyo | Rutland, Vermont | Singapore

We dedicate this book to our parents, Carmen and Nathaniel Simpkins and Naomi and Herbert Minkin, and to our children, Alura L, Aguilera and C. Alexander Simpkins Jr., and to all the dedicated Zen masters whose lives and actions help communicate Zen to us today.

Content

Introduction

The issues and themes of Taoism originated within contexts that were time-bound, situation-bound and culture-bound. So we presented the early figures and history simply, as sources of the key themes of Taoism. Taoism transcends its beginnings when its principles are applied in the moment. Taoism is a way to think and live. The principles apply just as much now in our modern context. Taoism's compass can help us find our way through life. The wise insights are timeless, and can light the path for our steps, giving us support in life's darker moments, comfort, balance and happiness in life's brighter times.

Taoism is an ancient philosophy whose wellspring is the unformed, unnameable, mystical guiding principle of Tao. Tao takes form as a pair of opposites, known as yin and yang, which, in turn, weave together and interrelate to create an infinite world of possibilities.

Although Taoism's basis is mystical, its application to life is practical. Taoism has inspired politics, philosophy, religion, medicine, art and science. In modern times, people are taught that if they try hard, they will succeed. This intense striving often leads to stress and discomfort. Taoists believe that you can accomplish more without effort, and Taoism reveals how to do this. You become one with Tao not to forget yourself, but to attune yourself to the rhythms of life so that you can develop your talents fully. Through this ancient philosophy, you discover a new way to calmness and creativity as well as strategies for living. You learn to succeed without seeming to even try.

Taoism blends well with other philosophies, such as Zen and Confucianism, providing an always available source of wisdom. Paradoxically, Taoism helps us to find light in the darkness of the unknown.

ABOUT THIS BOOK

This volume is designed to help you understand what Taoism is and how to put it to practical use in your life. *Taoism for Beginners* is divided into three parts. Part 1 gives the history and development of the philosophy, illustrated with stories to bring it to life. A timeline is included in the back of the book for quick reference. Part 2 explains key concepts, crystallizing Taoist principles, which interrelate in circularity, true to Taoism's values. Part 3 shows ways to bring the insights of this time-honored Eastern philosophy into your life so that you can live the wisdom for yourself!

PART I

Taoism in Time

*I seem a strange misty form. Like vapor I pass into the being
of others, and they, passing within me, become my guests.*
—Radhakamal Mukherjee

Taoism's history is obscure. The mist of time covers the beginnings
so that only vague, shadowy outlines can be seen. Its founding
fathers are enigmatic figures whose biographies are filled with legend, allegory, and mythical events. Their lifespans are said to be
long, well over one hundred years. Some are believed never to have
died, but to be living quietly among us as immortals. Taoism
evolved from a vast collection of practices and beliefs, interwoven
with additional concepts into the radiant tapestry we know today
as Taoism. Surely, the spirits of these ancient masters are still with
us, having an effect on the world! Hidden in shadows, their mysterious influence continues. They only pretended to die.

1
Origins and Background

There is in the Changes the Great Primal Beginning
(Tai Chi). This generates the two primary forces.
The two primary forces generate the four images.
The four images generate the eight trigrams.
—*I Ching*, Chapter 11

Much of what is known of early Chinese philosophies comes from the work of two famous historians, father and son, Ssu-ma Tan and his son Ssu-ma Ch'ien (145–86 B.C.E.). Ssu-ma Tan was the historian of the Royal Library. Ssu-ma Ch'ien wrote an extensive history entitled *Records of the Historian*. The records and writings of these two men have helped historians through the ages piece together the often vague background of China's great philosophies.

EARLY BELIEFS

The foundation of Chinese thought is the belief in a single cosmic universe, a Oneness with no beginning or end. Older than any of the schools of Chinese philosophy were certain basic beliefs that helped the Chinese understand themselves in relation to the world: in the beginning, the world was an endless void called Wu Chi. It was pictured as an empty circle formed by dotted lines. From this arose activity, expressed as yang and shown as an empty circle, and inactivity, expressed as yin, and shown as a black circle. The interactions of activity and inactivity are called *tai chi*, shown as the famous yin-yang circle, half black and half white.

I CHING, THE BOOK OF CHANGES

If all is one undivided cosmic universe of dynamic forces, then seers could help rulers predict and interpret those forces. To accomplish this, a system of divination gradually developed with a theory of how the universe goes through its cycles of change. Using an extraordinary handbook, passed down over the centuries, the *I Ching* (the Book of Changes), experts commented on the diagrams it contained to interpret the present, predict the future, and guide behavior in helpful ways. The original author is unknown, but the *I Ching* is considered a primary book of Confucianism and was also incorporated into Taoist thought.

From the vast mysterious cosmic universe, the One, all emerges. As this Oneness manifests in the world it divides into two: yin and yang. These dynamic opposites are represented as a yielding, broken—line for yin and a solid, firm line—for yang. The *I Ching* combined these lines in patterns which were used for divination. There are four possible ways to arrange these lines in pairs: two solid lines, two broken lines, one solid over a broken line, and one broken over a solid line.

Trigrams, combinations of three lines in a column, were thought to correspond to certain qualities of nature and the inner workings of the universe. The lines were first arranged as trigrams by Emperor Fu Hsi (2852–2738 B.C.E.). He saw the patterns on the shells of tortoises, which were commonly used as oracles. The two extremes, Ch'ien (three solid lines), Creative, and K'un (three broken lines), Receptive, were thought to represent the dynamics of heaven and earth. Ch'ien was the creative element, the ruler, the father, the light. K'un was the receptive principle, the mother, ruled from above, the dark. All the other trigrams were combinations of these two opposites.

The eight trigrams were combined into sixty-four possible hexagrams. By interpreting all the different patterns, the Chinese developed a way of predicting the likely course of events if things followed according to nature. The *I Ching's* elaborate science of divination predicted with uncanny accuracy.

This theory became the basis for Chinese natural science. Lunar calendars, developed as early as 1200 B.C.E., the Chinese tradition of healing with herbs and acupuncture are also rooted in this theory.

CHI AND ANCESTRAL SPIRITS

The ancient Chinese believed that the universe was *chi*. To them, everything in the world was far more than its biological, corporeal being. All was energy, or chi, a vital force in the universe that could be utilized in all facets of life. Chinese medicine, martial arts, and creative arts are all based in the proper raising and directing of chi. Like a river, chi should keep flowing.

Also part of the belief of the ancient Chinese was that when people died, part of them went down into the earth, but their spirits lived on in the Heavens as chi to become One with the cosmos. All people, alive and dead, then, were thought to be part of the universal energy. This allowed the living to be in touch with their ancestors through worship, rituals, and ceremonies. Ancestors could continue to influence life on earth, thereby perpetuating the interaction. Ancestors were actively involved in the ongoing, everyday lives of their descendants. And the lives of their descendants influenced them.

Time was not linear, as we think of it in the West, with a beginning, a middle, and an end. Time was an overlapping series of circles, a continuum of shifting cycles. Death was not an ending but rather a step in the continuum of time, with the potential for higher status as an ancestral spirit. Natural and supernatural forces were also in continuous flux, acting upon the spiritual and material universe. Boundaries were fluid, elastic, permeable.

THE FIVE ELEMENTS

All that we encounter is made up of five elements that the Chinese believed basic to life: water, wood, metal, earth, and fire. Because they perceived that the entire universe was in flux, always shifting, the elements were also always shifting through their interactions with one another. Some interactions were complementary, others were contending. For example, wood produces fire, making a complementary pair, whereas water puts out fire, making those two elements a contending pair. If we look at the world around us, we can see how the elements shift. We can observe destructive cycles—for example, when water evaporates or wood decomposes. But concomitantly, there is a regenerative cycle, during which water condenses and new trees grow. The Chinese believed that things do exist, but that existence is time-limited within the cycles of inevitable change.

THE SIX SCHOOLS

Chinese philosophies are based on the principles of Oneness and continual change. Each of these many philosophies developed their early principles in different directions, guiding people in how to lead healthy and happy lives.

During the last third of the Chou dynasty (approximately 551–221 B.C.E.), numerous philosophies emerged, known as the One Hundred Philosophies. Ssu-ma Tan classified these One Hundred Philosophies into six schools.

The Literati, or Scholar School, was exemplified by Confucius. The followers of the school were devoted to study and learning. They believed that the Way of morality and virtue could be cultivated and developed by education and correct practice.

The members of the School of Mo-tzu adhered to his doctrine of universal love. This was the first school to oppose Confucius. The School of Names looked for the distinctions between names and things. The Legalist School believed in fixed codes of law and government rather than morality and virtue as a solution to the world's problems.

The Yin Yang School derived from the principle of opposites. Yin is female and yang is male. The dynamic interplay of these polarities was fundamental to the manifestation of all phenomena in the world. Occult practices developed from this school and eventually merged with Taoism. The Taoist School was based in the Way and its power, natural virtue, and morality. The Way for the Taoist School was to follow Tao. What this was and how to do it unfolds here in this book.

2
Lao-Tzu:
Illuminating the Classic Way

The ancient sages never put their teachings in systematic form. They spoke in paradoxes, for they were afraid of uttering half-truths. They began by talking like fools and ended by making their hearers wise.
—Kakuzo Okakura, *The Book of Tea*

Historians have been trying to sort out fact from fiction regarding the development of Taoism. Some consensus exists on how it came to be and who were its pivotal figures, but because of different historical traditions and the nature of Taoism itself, much remains unknown.

Lao-tzu (born in 604 B.C.E.), the legendary author of the famous little book *Tao Te Ching*, was a man whose life was shrouded in mystery. According to legend, he was conceived when his mother admired a falling star. He matured in her womb for sixty-two years. One day, she leaned against a plum tree and gave birth to a full-grown man with white hair and long earlobes (a symbol of wisdom). He named himself after the plum tree (*Li*) and proclaimed his first name to be Ear (*Erh*). Much of the literature refers to him as Li Erh, or Lao Tan, but more often he is called Lao-tzu, meaning old master.

The earliest mention of Lao-tzu's biography was in Ssu-ma

Ch'ien's *Records of the Historian*. Ssu-ma Ch'ien recorded that Lao-tzu was a native of the hamlet of Ch'u-jen, village of Li, in the state of Ch'en, which, in 479 B.C.E., became part of the state of Ch'u. Both Lao-tzu and Confucius lived in this area.

Lao-tzu worked in the capital city of Loyang as the Keeper of the Archives for the royal court of Chou. This position gave him access to the classic texts that were kept in the royal archives, which was like a library. He was familiar with the lore of the Yellow Emperor (2697 B.C.E.) and all the great works of the time. He was about fifty years older than Confucius, who was said to have consulted Lao-tzu for information on rituals.

This famous meeting between Lao-tzu and Confucius was described by Ssu-ma Ch'ien. During the encounter, Confucius asked Lao-tzu, "Please instruct me on the proper rites for behavior."

Lao-tzu answered, "A person may have all the outward appearances of a gentleman when times are good. But if he encounters hard times, he will drift like the wind. A true gentleman hides his wealth; the man of superior virtue has the outward appearance of a fool! Throw away your arrogant rituals! None of them have any relevance to our true self. That is my advice to you!" Confucius was impressed. He said, "The dragon is beyond my knowledge; it ascends into the heaven on the cloud and the wind. Today I have seen Lao-tzu, and he is like the dragon!"

Tradition holds that Lao-tzu married and had a son named Tsung, who became a well-known soldier. Many later generations trace themselves back to Lao-tzu. This may or may not be accurate, but it attests to the fact that he was given great symbolic importance in Chinese history.

It is believed that Lao-tzu never opened a formal school, but students still came to him and he had a number of loyal disciples. If these statements about Lao-tzu are true, he led a fairly busy and full life.

Eventually, however, Lao-tzu felt frustrated by the moral decay of the society around him. City life did not allow him to live in harmony with his Taoist beliefs. At the ripe old age of 160 years, he decided to leave the city for the unsettled west to live a solitary life as a hermit. He began his trip westward, leaving through the city gate. The gatekeeper recognized him and begged Lao-tzu to leave some record of his wisdom. In response, Lao-tzu sat down and composed the five-thousand-character book now known as the *Tao Te Ching*. The gatekeeper was so moved by its content that he decided to accompany Lao-tzu. The two disappeared together, never to be seen again. One legend claims that Lao-tzu reappeared in India to convert the Buddha. Another story alleges that Lao-tzu was the Buddha!

Facts fuse with myth regarding Lao-tzu. Researchers through the ages have debated whether he actually wrote the *Tao Te Ching*, or if he was even a real person. Perhaps it has been difficult to verify the facts of Lao-tzu's life because of the ancient Chinese belief that it was dishonorable to write one's autobiography. Better to wait until death and hope that someone would do the honor! Lao-tzu was given a high position by later generations. Some Taoists considered him a deity, and built a temple on the site of his birthplace. In many areas throughout China there are Taoist temples, much like the many Buddhist temples.

Lao-tzu was deeply mystical. He believed that the Tao is the source, the inner axis of the universe. The inner nature of the world is mysterious, prior to name and form. That which can be given a name is not Tao.

TAO TE CHING

No book other than the Bible has been translated and read more than the *Tao Te Ching*. What draws so many people to this enigmatic book are the deep meanings that can be culled from its profound words. This book expresses the essence of early Taoist philosophy. Composed as short, poetic chapters, the words, written in ancient Chinese characters, are laden with possible interpretations. Thus, each translator becomes interpreter, with a seemingly endless variety of understandings, yet we can hear resonance in themes that echo throughout. Like a haunting melody transposed into different keys, the Taoist principles can be heard again and again.

The *Tao Te Ching* (Classic of the Way and Its Virtue) is divided into two parts, one on Tao, the mysterious Oneness that guides everyone and everything, and the other on Te, the power that is achieved by following Tao, totaling eighty-two chapters. The *Tao Te Ching* points to the Taoist Way and shows how following it will lead to a fulfilling life. Lao-tzu chose to express the Tao through ambiguous, poetic verse that could awaken the intuition of Tao in his readers. He did not presume to communicate its concepts through clearly defined words, for words hide the Tao. Inner essences, to Lao-tzu, are neither communicated nor reflected in words. But then, perhaps that is best; when it is hidden, it is revealed. Communication is more than words.

LAO-TZU'S CONCEPTS

Lao-tzu's *Tao Te Ching* expresses concepts that interrelate systematically to give meaning and a basis for understanding. Forces create one another through chain reactions initiated by the energies of opposites. Events in the real world are the result of these forces. Even as a pattern comes into being, it vanishes. Being and nonbeing are only aspects of each other, mutually caused.

Tao is bottomless yet empty, the heart of things, of life. Immortality is found in the emptiness. From the emptiness springs usefulness. The empty space within a cup is what makes a cup useful, for without any empty space within, a cup cannot be filled.

Tao is the source, older than nature. Nature is rooted in Tao. Everything that we know in the world comes from Tao, expressed as yin and yang. Thus, anything we do will invariably create its own opposite. To succeed in life according to Lao-tzu, we should step back and permit this balancing to take place. The situations of life seem to be one way, but they quickly assert their dual nature. The sage encourages contentment by letting go of excess desires. Simplicity leads to freedom from desire.

Wisdom lies in not contending. Sensitive to the inner nature of self and other, Lao-tzu's Way leads through mystery, by returning to the core of life. When you let be, circumstances stop being a problem. They go through their cycle. Allow matters to take their natural course, and the struggle of resistance lessens. Everything is then taken care of by its own patterns of activation and rest. Yin and yang represent the natural polarity that inevitably arises. By encouraging the natural, the sage permits Tao to become manifest. Thus, wisdom is found in silence, in quiet, in letting be. This draws things into being.

3
Chuang-Tzu: Tales of Tao

Is not he who preserves the body and gives the fullest development to the life, who establishes the attributes of the Tao and clearly displays It, possessed of kingly qualities?
–Chuang-tzu

Chuang-tzu (369–286 B.C.E.) stands with Lao-tzu as one of the most wellknown and prolific founders of Taoism. His works, known as *The Chuang-tzu*, elucidate and illustrate Taoist concepts through colorful stories. Chuang-tzu's writings deeply inspired Chinese philosophical, medical, and aesthetic theory in general and tai chi chuan and Zen Buddhism in particular. Zen teachers use his concepts and metaphors to convey principles that parallel those of Zen.

Chuang-tzu's real name was Chuang Chou. *Tzu* means master and is a title of respect, and thus he is best known as Chuang-tzu, Master Chuang. Little is known about his personal life outside of his writings and a short biography, compiled by the historian Ssuma Ch'ien. Chuang-tzu grew up and lived in the state of Meng, part of the kingdom of Wei, where Lao-tzu spent most of his life. He was a contemporary of the famous Confucian scholar, Mencius, who wrote, "The words of Chuang-tzu and Mo-tzu fill the world."

Chuang-tzu was well versed in the prominent philosophies of his day, along with the classics, but he made his preference for

Taoism very clear. Unlike other Taoist writers, Chuang-tzu's work takes issue with all other philosophies, especially Confucianism. He wrote numerous stories in which Taoist sages convince philosophers from other schools of Taoism's wisdom. One of his favorite scenarios is in the form of dialogues between Confucius and Lao-tzu. Confucius, the younger man, questions Lao-tzu as if he were addressing a wise sage. In the end, Confucius is convinced that Taoism is in harmony with a profound truth that can enhance his Confucianist beliefs.

In a typical encounter, Confucius went to Lao-tzu and said, "I have read the *Six Classics* and consider myself an expert. Yet none of the seventy-two rulers whom I advise have ever put my ideas into practice! What am I doing wrong?"

Lao-tzu answered, "You may have read the *Six Classics*, but keep in mind that these are only footprints, not the shoes themselves. Look at nature. Each animal reproduces according to its nature. Some are live bearers, others lay eggs, to give you a few examples. Every species has its own nature and that nature cannot be altered! The Tao cannot be stopped. When you have the Tao there isn't anything that you can't do, but if you don't have it, you can't do anything!"

Confucius spent the next three months alone in his house, meditating on Lao-tzu's words. When he returned to visit the Master, he told him, "I have it now! I understand that each animal reproduces in its own unique way in accordance with its own nature. I have my own part in the harmony. When I did not teach the rulers in harmony with the natural way, how could I expect to change them?"

Lao-tzu replied, "Now you have got it!" (Paraphrased from *Chuang-tzu*, Chapter 15). Thus, Lao-tzu helped Confucius learn to guide his actions by the hidden essence, not by external knowledge.

THE IMPORTANCE OF INNER FREEDOM

Chuang-tzu lived his philosophy, consistent with his principles. He was protective of his time and freedom and therefore chose a simple governmental job that left him plenty of time for fishing and philosophy. He had a small number of disciples who spent time with him in philosophical discussions, and he never let any of his professional endeavors compromise his self-determination.

One of the most famous stories about Chuang-tzu shows how much he valued life and freedom. King Wei of Chu heard about Chuang-tzu's ability to express profound concepts with clarity and wit. One day the king sent messengers laden with gifts to invite Chuang-tzu to his court and offer him the position of prime minister. The messengers found Chuang-tzu quietly fishing. In a proud voice, the messenger said, "You have been honored by our king. He extends to you an invitation to become his minister."

Chuang-tzu continued to fish. Then he smiled and said thoughtfully, "I am honored that the king would like to hire me for such an esteemed position as prime minister. But before I give you my answer, let me ask you a question. I have heard that the prince of Chu keeps a sacred tortoise who lived three thousand years carefully enclosed in a chest on the altar. Now I ask you, would that tortoise rather be dead and have his remains viewed and revered in a museum, or do you think he would prefer to be alive and splashing in the mud?"

The messengers could not help but answer, "Of course, the tortoise would rather be alive, playing in the mud."

Chuang-tzu answered, "Then leave me now. I would rather be free to splash in the mud!" Chuang-tzu believed that people will live happy and satisfying lives if they are free to develop. He thought that each individual must be allowed to journey unhindered through the cycles of life.

RELATIVE KNOWLEDGE VS. THE ABSOLUTE WISDOM OF TAO

When the distinctions of true and false appeared, then Tao lost its wholeness. And when Tao lost its wholeness, individual bias began.
—Lao-tzu

Chuang-tzu felt that people spent too much time disputing back and forth about every aspect of living. Too much talking takes people away from the Tao. "Words are [like] waves acted on by the wind," he said, "the real point of the matters is lost." Chuang-tzu lived during an unstable period in Chinese history, when people were continually disputing politics and philosophy. He believed that all of these arguments were relative. People argue because they have lost touch with the unity underlying the apparent distinctions: Tao precedes any differences.

Looked at through Tao, all perspectives are equal. Everything is part of the unity. Tao eludes any restrictive definition. It is everything and everywhere, the grounds and basis of wisdom. Lao-tzu pointed out that the person who thinks he knows does not really know, but the one who knows what he does not know is wise. Wisdom comes from inner intuition, the deeper nature of things. Opinion, knowledge, and learning are only impediments to wisdom. The Tao can never be found in worldly things. Chuang-tzu advised people to stay at peace with nature in order to truly know.

Throughout his writings, Chuang-tzu illustrated many of his points with examples from nature. He believed that the Way of nature is the Way of Tao. When nature is encouraged to thrive and permitted to follow its path without interference, it will develop just as it should. Each is uniquely suited to its own lifeworld. People should not try to impose their own design. Instead, they should find the inner pattern, and follow it. Artists should paint or draw spontaneously from nature, and creative inspiration will follow. Sometimes the inner pattern can only be known in terms of what it is not. Rejection of education and culturally learned limitations may be the necessary first step. The glow of true nature within can brighten the darkness of the unknown. The leap of intuition is more than a first step; it actually guides us on our journey. Reason, paradoxically, leads us astray.

Chuang-tzu explained with an example about horses. Horses' hoofs allow them to travel over frost and snow and hair on their bodies to withstand wind and cold. It is part of their nature to eat grass, drink water, and run through the countryside. Human beings came along and altered this. They trimmed the horses' mane, shoed their hoofs, and placed yokes around their necks. Under such externally imposed patterns, horses are restricted to a narrow path and cannot thrive. These human actions disrupt the natural order of things. Thus, Chuang-tzu encouraged his students not to seek to be useful, lest they become unknowingly enchained while losing touch with their spontaneous inner nature. Uselessness has its use. Set yourself free, Chuang-tzu advised.

RETURN TO THE PRIMITIVE

Let all of earth's creatures, including people, live in accordance with their nature, and everyone will prosper. All are part of the Tao, expressing Tao by their own individual way of living. Chuang-tzu believed that each person has his or her own gifts and individual talents to express. When people follow their path, nature shows them the Way. They cannot fail. As problems arise, solutions emerge. Return to your origins in the primitive for wisdom. Problems are only apparent, arising from mistaking relative existence for absolute Tao.

In a famous story recounted by Chuang-tzu, Prince Yuan of Sung was seeking a painter. He asked all applicants to come to the palace at a certain time of day. All arrived, neat and punctual, at the appointed time except for one man, who wandered in dressed casually, quite late. The palace guards turned the strange, uncouth artist away, and he returned to his lodgings. The prince, however, became curious and wanted to see what the man could do. He sent some messengers to the artist's room. When they arrived and asked to see the artist, he removed all his clothes and squatted down in a corner of the room. The messengers returned to the prince and described the strange behavior. "Bring him to me!" the prince said. "He is a true painter." This partakes of the essence of Taoist art: naked, primitive, spontaneous, without concern for decoration through outer appearance or garments. Through art, the artist expresses his individual chi, the inner life force.

How, then, do we learn to follow our own true nature? Chuang-tzu's answer is reminiscent of Buddhism in that the best technique to find Tao is through meditation, through learning to be empty of thoughts and desires. But Taoism interprets this a little differently from Buddhism: Practice self-forgetfulness. By self-abandonment to the realm of the unknown, the inner pattern will emerge. By acting spontaneously in synchrony with inner patterns, correct conduct is found. Then you can live unhindered by anything external. Return to the source of your life, the foundation in the wordless, unfathomable, unknowable Tao, and you will discover your true nature.

THE IMPORTANCE OF DREAMS

Chuang-tzu stretches the limits of "unknowing" to question our very certainty about consciousness. How do we know if we are truly awake? Chuang-tzu dreamt he was a butterfly, fluttering about happily in nature. He knew only that world of experience. The dream seemed real. When he awoke, he remembered his dream and knew he was Chuang-tzu. Then he wondered was he Chuang-tzu awake, remembering his dream of being a butterfly, or was he actually only a butterfly, asleep, dreaming he was a man, awake? Are we asleep or awake?

For Chuang-tzu, the unconscious dream state could not be distinguished from the waking, conscious state of mind. Tao can be found anywhere, at any time. But perhaps through dreams we are less impeded by conscious limits. These ideas were developed by Lieh-tzu (see Chapter 4) and can be put to use to help foster self-discovery (see Chapter 17).

FINAL YEARS

When Chuang-tzu was old and knew he was soon going to die, his disciples offered to give him a large, impressive funeral to show their great respect and love for him. Chuang-tzu protested and said, "I shall have heaven and earth for my coffin, the sun and moon for my two round symbols of jade, and the stars and constellations as my jewels. Isn't that more than anyone could possibly want?"

The disciples responded, "But we are afraid that the crows will eat you, Master."

Chuang-tzu smiled at them benevolently and said, "Above, the crows will eat me. Below, the moles and ants will eat me. To give to these and take from those would only show your one-sidedness. All are equal under the Tao." These were the last words of Chuang-tzu, a man who wholeheartedly devoted his entire life to the Taoist Way.

4
Lieh-Tzu and Yang Chu: Traveling the Path

"The virtue of Heaven and Earth, the powers of the Sage, and the uses of the myriad things in Creation, are not perfect in every direction. It is Heaven's function to produce life and to spread a canopy over it. It is Earth's function to form material bodies and to support them. It is the Sage's function to teach others and to influence them for good."
—Lieh-tzu

Lieh-tzu was a Taoist whose writings expressed the fundamentals of Taoism as a guide to action and for inspiration. The *Book of Lieh-tzu* helped add to the foundation of classical Taoist literature that breathes life into Taoist philosophy. Some of the stories in the *Book of Lieh-tzu* overlap with Chuang-tzu's accounts. These stories are part of Taoism's traditional teachings. Lieh-tzu reinterpreted other Chinese philosophies in Taoist terms, finding principles of the Tao in all things, unifying later thinkers with the Taoists.

Lieh-tzu's given name was Lieh Yu-K'ou (or K'an). He lived in the state of Cheng, and eventually moved to Wei. His teacher was Hu-tzu (Hu Ch'iu Lin). Lieh-tzu was referred to by Mencius, Chuang-tzu and others, showing that he was well-known around the third century B.C.E.

Lieh-tzu's authenticity has been disputed at different times through history, but many modern scholars believe he did exist. It is uncertain whether Lieh-tzu personally authored the *Book of Lieh-tzu*. In keeping with early Chinese tradition, his writings were probably gathered later by his disciples. The book that is ascribed to Lieh-tzu is likely a compilation from more than one author rendering Lieh-tzu's thoughts. Thus, the ideas were from an early historical period, probably around 398 B.C.E., but were compiled later.

As further support for the theory that Lieh-tzu's book may have been written later, the work makes peace and comes to terms with other theories. Confucius is treated respectfully as is Mo-tzu, embraced as expressing Tao. The *I Ching* is also reinterpreted within Taoism's concepts. This trend toward unification developed even further, and by the time of the Neo-Taoists (220–420 C.E.), Confucius was lauded as the greatest of all sages. *The Book of Lieh-tzu* helped bridge the gap between Taoism and other philosophies.

LIEH-TZU'S IDEAS

Like Lao-tzu and Chuang-tzu, Lieh-tzu believed in the intuitive attunement to Tao—wordless, still, calm, unrestrained, simple. He encouraged people to trust nature and find balance, both within and without. This lifestyle leads to the life of Tao—uninhibited, creative, and free.

Like Chuang-tzu, Lieh-tzu believed that everything that is created flows in a cycle, from birth and growth to death and decay. The natural cycles are inevitable. "Going forth and returning, its successions are endless."

EFFORT AND DESTINY

We act, and the fruits
Of our actions
Ripen, to
Become, to be
Borne on winds of destiny
—C. Alexander Simpkins

Two sets of forces are always acting upon our lives: human effort and destiny. Our own efforts bring about many things—professional development, mastery of a skill. Destiny, however, the more powerful force, can strike at any point to alter our path. The sage knows that it is futile to fight against destiny. Lieh-tzu advised his readers to ally themselves with destiny. Then they will live in tune with Tao and find themselves naturally developing their destiny to its fullest potential.

LIFE IS BUT A DREAM

Things come into being from Tao, then differentiate into various combinations of yin and yang. One manifestation of yin and yang is between reality and illusion. Light always produces shadow. Sound produces echo. We are always in a relationship between concrete reality and the illusory, mystical realm of shadows, echoes, and dreams. Lieh-tzu explains through many stories that Chuang-tzu's question—Am I a man dreaming I am a butterfly, or a butterfly dreaming I am a man—should be explored.

Lieh-tzu tells a story about a poor servant who was overworked by his master. Every night the servant fell into an exhausted sleep and dreamed that he was lord over a vast kingdom with all the wealth and leisure he desired. Despite his hard life, the servant was happy. When asked how he could possibly find joy in such an unpleasant life, he answered, "Even though my waking hours are toil and discomfort, I spend the sleeping half of my life in abundant joy!"

Meanwhile, the master of the household passed his waking hours plagued by worries about his household and the distribution of his wealth. At night he, too, fell into an exhausted sleep, but he dreamed he was a slave, driven to toil at hard labor. A friend advised him that his negative dreams were destiny's balancing for his cruel treatment of his servant. Recognizing the truth in these words, the master lightened his servant's load and eased his personal worries. His dreams and waking hours became more comfortable and fulfilling.

Taoist sages often guided people toward more fulfilling and healthier lives through dreams and illusion. Lieh-tzu told a story of how the Yellow Emperor became great. This mythical emperor was believed to have reigned wisely over China thousands of years before Christ. According to the story, his empire was not always happy and prosperous. For many years the kingdom experienced difficulties, and no matter what he did, nothing improved. One night he dreamt that he traveled to a particular kingdom that functioned perfectly without a leader. The Yellow Emperor realized when he woke up that he needed to alter his ruling methods. He stopped interfering and fostered his people's development. From then on, his kingdom thrived.

The Taoist sages were equally comfortable in the dream state as in the waking state. In traditional legends, they gained the freedom to perform impossible feats, such as walking through walls and flying through the air, by embracing and identifying with the magical, illusory essence. Many of the miraculous actions that were attributed to Taoist immortals can be understood by accepting the importance of the unconscious, dreaming mind.

YANG CHU

Yang Chu is another important early Taoist sage. Yang Chu's values and concepts are referred to consistently by other philosophers. Some scholars believe he lived early, others place him later. Only a few fragmentary references remain, unlike the works of Lao-tzu, Chuang-tzu, and Lieh-tzu. The *Book of Lieh-tzu* has a chapter—"Yang Chu"—in which Yang Chu's teachings are described through various narrative accounts. Some translators dispute the authenticity of this chapter and leave it out of the *Book of Lieh-tzu*. The renowned 20th century scholar-historian of Chinese philosophy Wing-tsit Chan does not even consider Yang Chu a true Taoist, but most scholars do. Later Taoism followed one or the other view. Yang Chu, however, is referred to by Lieh-tzu throughout his writings, illustrating Taoist responses to situations that could epitomize the Way.

Yang Chu's principles are clear. He encourages his students to live freely, spontaneously, without conscious interference—according to Tao. This may be practiced by a highly achieving member of the privileged class or by an underachieving vagabond. When asked what was the correct course for life, Yang Chu answered:

It is to be found in enjoying life, in freeing ourselves from care. Hence, those who are good at enjoying life are not poor, and those who are good at freeing themselves from care do not become rich.

No principle or rule can be given to guide behavior: Every rule or principle is one-sided and faulty. Tao is the only possible guide, before rules and words, at peace, the supreme rule. Yang Chu represented freedom from rules, freedom to be spontaneous, to preserve life, to follow impulse and satisfy yourself, rather than live according to sober rules. In permitting self-expression, Yang

Chu believed, life is fulfilled.

Yang Chu is sometimes derogated as a hedonist based on a particular passage in the Yang Chu chapter. In this passage Yang Chu is asked if he could help the whole world by sacrificing one hair on his head, would he do it? Yang Chu's answer was no, because he believed that valuing life should come before all other concerns. If life is cultivated, "tending life" as he called it, then all else would fall into place as it should.

The Neo-Taoists followed Yang Chu's direction, as exemplified by the Seven Sages of the Bamboo Grove, who allowed their impulses free rein (see Chapter 5).

5
Neo-Taoists:
Feelings and Thoughts Evolve

But when one wishes to enjoy himself in the fullest and freest
way, he must first have before him a view like that of the
wide sea or the expanse of the air, in order that his mind
may be free from restraint, and that it may respond in
the fitting way to everything coming before it:—it is only
what is Great that can enter into this enjoyment.
—Lin Hsi-kung

The Neo-Taoists were a group of intellectuals living from 220 to 420 C.E., during a period when philosophy was dominated by Confucianism. The Neo-Taoists turned back to the classic Taoists, Lao-tzu and Chuang-tzu along with the *I Ching*, reinterpreting the original Taoist themes and blending them with Confucianism. Neo-Taoism was also affected by Buddhism, which was spreading rapidly throughout China. Zen Buddhism, not to be founded for another hundred years, would also be influenced by Neo-Taoist principles.

The Neo-Taoists tended to be idealistic youths, many of them scholars. They engaged in what they called "Pure Conversation," or *ch'ing t'an*. They tried to express themselves as fully authentic and sensitive individuals. They considered each conversation a sublime meeting of souls. Some historians have compared their ideals to the Beats of the 1950s, with a similar commitment to being themselves and freely expressing their inner nature. These young seekers searched for ultimate reality, true understanding in happy dialogues, standing apart from what they considered the corrupting influence of striving for personal gain.

SEVEN WORTHIES OF THE BAMBOO GROVE

One famous group of Neo-Taoists was known as the Seven Worthies of the Bamboo Grove. They met in a grove of bamboo to discuss metaphysics, read poetry, often drinking heavily, and behaving whimsically. Their way was aptly termed *feng lin*, "wandering from convention." Yang-chu's writings can be seen as an inspiration for these free-spirited philosophers. One of the members, Liu Ling (221–300) was a heavy drinker and a nudist within his house. One day a visitor came to his door and was shocked to find Liu Ling without clothing. Liu Ling responded to the visitor's surprise and said, "I take the whole universe as my house and my own room as my clothing. Get out of my trousers!" The embarrassed visitor fled.

The Neo-Taoists were spontaneous and uninhibited. Wang Hui-chih woke up in the middle of the night after a heavy snowfall and suddenly thought of his friend Tai. He immediately left his house and took an all-night boat ride to the house of this friend. Just as he reached Tai's doorstep, he turned around and went home. Later, someone asked him why he had done this. Wang Hui-chih answered with self-assurance, "I came on the impulse of my pleasure, and now it is ended, so I go back. Why should I see Tai?" Freely expressing his impulses paradoxically released Wang Hui-chih from the chains of determined action. The Neo-Taoists brought Taoism from thought into action.

Wang Pi (226–249) was a prominent Neo-Taoist who wrote commentaries on Lao-tzu and the *I Ching* that reinterpreted these classic texts. He lived a short but intense life, dying at the young age of twenty-four. Wang Pi and the other Neo-Taoists introduced this new movement.

WU-WEI IS FEELING AND DOING WHAT IS NATURAL

The Neo-Taoists justified their sometimes unconventional behavior in part because of their innovative interpretation of nonaction. They considered *wu-wei*, nonactivity, as natural, and added a new complementary concept, *yu-wei*, as a counterbalance. Yu-wei was activity that they believed to be unnatural. When people follow their natural tendencies they are wu-wei, but if they try to force themselves to do things, they are yu-wei. Chuang-tzu idealized the return to the primitive noble savage. The Neo-Taoists reinterpreted this concept of "primitive" to mean authentic or sincere. Being who you are and permitting your life force to be expressed fully with genuineness was of utmost importance: "If by primitive we mean the undistorted, the man whose character is not distorted is the most primitive, though he may be capable of doing many things."

The Neo-Taoists took a different position on emotions. The classical Taoists counseled stillness and quietism to enhance Taoist wisdom. The Neo-Taoist believed that feeling and expressing emotions would make them wiser. They explained that sages quieted their minds, seeking to be one with Tao. But as a human being, a sage would, at times, feel emotions of anger or joy like other people. The difference between a wise Taoist and an unenlightened person is that sages could have their feeling without becoming trapped or hindered by their emotional responses. Many modern forms of experiential psychotherapy embrace a similar insight. When you become one with your feelings, by experiencing and accepting them as part of your natural responses, your emotions transform. You are free to choose your actions in response. As Wang Pi expressed it, "The sage has emotions but no ensnarement."

In order to feel their emotions, the Neo-Taoists developed perceptual sensitivity. They were sensitive not only to personal circumstances but also to the world around them. Their feelings about the beauty of nature intensified. They noticed things that other people ignored. They sought refined aesthetic experiences, seeking to be connoisseurs of life. Those who achieved this were said to have refined their personality. The Neo-Taoists respected and appreciated a natural, genuine, well-developed personality.

The Neo-Taoists were not against learning. They believed that great writers and thinkers like Plato and Chuang-tzu were being authentic by writing philosophical books. This was their true nature, to be thoughtful writers. Thus, any kind of learning or emotion that is natural to the person can be positive.

REINTERPRETATION OF CONFUCIUS

The Neo-Taoists broadened the scope of the practical-minded Confucian doctrines that had been influencing thought for several centuries by including metaphysical questions about being and nonbeing. Chuang-tzu and Lao-tzu had emphasized the Way of Nature, but the Neo-Taoists talked about the Principle of Nature. They did not reject Confucianism; they examined it in terms of Taoism.

The Neo-Taoists believed that Confucius was even greater than Lao-tzu and Chuang-tzu, viewing him as the master of emptiness. They justified Confucius's concern with everyday life, rituals, ceremonies, and external circumstances by arguing that he realized that it is impossible to instruct directly about *wu*, nonbeing, emptiness. Therefore, he wisely focused all his attention on *yu*, being. This explanation reflects the idea expressed by Lao-tzu: "He who knows does not speak; he who speaks, does not know" (*Tao Te Ching*, Chapter 56). By not even speaking of Tao in his sayings, Confucius was the ultimate Taoist.

The Neo-Taoists believed what the *I Ching* stated: Everything is continually changing, never still. They encouraged people to accept change. The old is different from the new, and even though tradition may have its place, people and institutions should change with the times. Unlike the early Taoists, these philosophers did not oppose all institutions or moral values, only those that were unwilling to evolve. This view permitted the Neo-Taoists to embrace useful principles in other philosophies. Taoism was modified considerably, opening the possibility for later philosophers to incorporate Taoist principles within Neo-Confucianism.

6

Later Developments Toward Health and Long Life

*What is preached should be put into practice—
only then is it called speech and action without defect.*
—Chang Po-tuan, *Understanding Reality*

The Taoist philosophy of Lao-tzu, Chuang-tzu, Lieh-tzu, and the Neo-Taoists is but one aspect of the larger body of Taoism that is practiced as a religion for both spiritual fulfillment and physical well-being. Taoist religions are a complex, vast collection of customs, rituals, and beliefs that have never been organized into one single, consistent set of doctrines. Rural areas were the stronghold of Taoist religions, surviving for more than two millennia in the hearts and minds of the people.

TAOIST RELIGION EMERGES

Religious Taoism began in separate groups that traced their inspiration back to Lao-tzu and concepts within the *Tao Te Ching*. Historians believe that Taoist religion is very old, incorporating primitive Chinese shamanic religions. Bronze and gold objects representing Taoist immortals have been found in tombs, dating early Taoist worship back to the third century B.C.E.

References to Taoist religion can be found in the writings of philosophical Taoists, especially Chuang-tzu and Lieh-tzu. Both refer to faraway places where divine beings lived free of all worldly limitations, capable of great powers. Lieh-tzu spoke of men who could walk through walls, implying that nothing in this world could stop them. Chuang-tzu described these godlike people in the very first book of his writings:

> *On the distant mountain of Ku-yeh live divine beings. . . . They mount clouds of ch'i and ride winged dragons to wander beyond the Four Seas. . . . By concentrating their minds, they can protect all beings from plague and ripen the crops. . . . These men! What power (te)! They embrace the Ten Thousand Beings, making them into a single one."*

Religious Taoism was implied in the early philosophical Taoist writers, but religious interpretations were made explicit by the beginning of the Christian era. The image and meaning of Lao-tzu transformed, much like Buddha's metamorphosis, from being thought of as a man of great insight to becoming a deity. Taoism merged with earlier mythologies and occult sciences. One such combination put Lao-tzu with Huang-ti, a mythological inventor who was worshiped by craftsmen and artisans. This unity was called Huang-Lao Chih Tao, the Way of the Yellow Emperor and the Old Master. Lao-tzu was worshiped and revered, now that he had risen to the status of a deity.

During the second Han dynasty, Lao-tzu's writings were believed to contain secret practices to prolong life using special forms of meditation. For example, certain passages from the *Tao Te Ching* refer to "nurturing the life principle." Such passages inspired Taoists to search for methods that would extend life and find immortality.

FOUNDING OF THE TAOIST CHURCH

The Taoist religion began as small sects established by charismatic healers who promised a better life through healthy, moral living. Among the practical principles to achieve this were diet and medicinal prescriptions. As they evolved, Taoist sects became political and social communities where people could live, work, and be taken care of.

The many sects were not interrelated, nor did they all share the same beliefs. The larger, more complex ones were more successful over time. Three major sects, all founded by people with the name Chang, sprang up around the second century C.E.

Chang Ling, born during the reign of Emperor Huan (147–167 C.E.) was the founder of the Heavenly Masters sect, one of the many health cults of the period. He was a missionary who studied ancient methods for achieving long life. He brought his ideas to the people of Szechwan Province, wrote a book about his methods, and gathered many converts. People were required to pay five bushels of rice when they joined, giving the sect its original name, Five Bushel sect. He took the title T'ien Chih, which means Heavenly Master. Eventually, the sect was known as the Heavenly (or Celestial) Masters sect.

Chang Ling's son Chang Heng took over the sect, and although he did not contribute anything new, his wife had connections with the governor of Chou, who gave the sect an army. The next generation of Changs, Chang Lu, used the army and a general named Chang Hsiu to make the organization grow and spread.

General Chang Hsiu separated from the Heavenly Masters to organize his own successful health cult. He believed that sickness was the result of sin, so treatment involved confession and repentance. Patients were sometimes forcibly kept in seclusion to contemplate their sins. They atoned for their sins by writing down penance on three sheets of paper, one to fly up to heaven, the second to dig under the earth, and the third to be cast into water. General Chang Hsiu's community was based on a hierarchical, military structure. Priests were also military leaders.

Eventually, the sects of Chang Lu and Chang Hsiu dominated a number of provinces. People living within these Taoist communities separated from the greater Chinese culture. More and more people joined as Taoism spread.

In a dark chapter of Taoism's history, Chang Lu decided to take over the general's sect. He had the general killed and became the leader of both sects. Ironically, he became a great proponent of many new doctrines, such as honesty and trustworthiness. He set up free inns for travelers where Taoism could be taught, a tradition that continued into the Tang period. The Heavenly Masters sect is still vital in modern China and Taiwan.

Another sect was founded by Yu Chi, a healer from the east who incorporated Five Elements Theory, sorcery, and medicine. He wrote his ideas in *T'ai Ping Ch'ing Ling Shu*, the Book of Grand Peace and Purity, but his career ended abruptly when he was murdered by a jealous ruler, the marquis of Wu. His message was carried on by a new movement, named after his book, the Way of Grand Peace, led by Chang Chueh. (no relation to the other Changs). The Heavenly Masters and the Grand Peace and Harmony sects evolved. Both had a strict hierarchy and favored public displays of repentance for transgressions.

As the ruling Han dynasty declined, it became cruel, and conditions for the average citizen were harsh. The impoverished people were forced to support the court's corrupt luxuries, leaving few resources for families to adequately feed themselves. The magical mists of Taoism swept through the country, promising power, health, and even immortality, all within a supportive community.

Most of China converted to Taoism by 184 C.E., with the exception of the area immediately surrounding the capital. The government felt threatened and warned that they would prohibit Taoism. In response, more than 350,000 people joined together and rose against the government as one, wearing yellow turbans on their heads. Their action became known as the Yellow Turban Rebellion. Although they were not ultimately victorious, the rebellion seriously weakened the crushing grip of the Han dynasty.

Taoist religion continued to develop and evolve. Leadership was passed down along family lines, and continued to be. The heads of modern Taoist sects are from this lineage, passed along father to son for hundreds of years.

IMMORTALITY

Many of the Taoist sects were seeking a similar goal: a long healthy life leading to immortality. Some attempted to physically transform their bodies so they could live forever, but for the most part, the immortality sought was spiritual. Practices were developed to help bring this about. Those who succeeded—the Immortals— were people who died—or seemed to—but when their coffins were later opened to make sure, their bodies could not be found. No longer of this earth, the Immortals roamed special heavens or supernatural islands such as P'eng-lai, a mystical Shangri-La.

Immortals could be men or women, even animals. One famous woman Immortal was named Hsi Wang Mu, Queen Mother of the West. White cranes have always had mythical qualities to the Chinese. These birds were thought to live for a thousand years. Their cinnabar-colored head proved they knew the secret of preserving life, since cinnabar was believed to bring immortality. Immortals were often pictured riding on the backs of cranes.

Immortality could also be spiritual. The body was gone, but great Taoist sages like Lao-tzu, Chuang-tzu, and others continued to speak and appear to Taoist practitioners. Some sects used automatic writing and mediums to communicate with these ancestral spirits, who were believed to have gained immortality of spirit.

TAOIST ALCHEMY

To age with the sun and moon and be renewed by spring and summer; to conserve the seeds of growth in autumn and winter and to be nourished by the eternal breath of the Tao—these are the goals of the Taoist.

—Dragon-Tiger Classic

Taoists not only searched for personal immortality, they also developed methods for enhancing and prolonging life. Early in Chinese history, around 200 B.C.E., magicians, known as *fang shih*, or "recipe gentlemen," were concocting alchemical mixtures for immortality. They experimented with elixirs based on cinnabar (mercuric sulfide), jade, and gold, mistakenly believing these minerals possessed life-giving properties. Special artifacts made of these materials became power objects, thought to hold the key to longevity. They crafted eating and drinking utensils with cinnabar, lead, and gold, which they believed could increase the life span of anyone who used them. Those foolish enough to consume elixirs or eat from instruments made from these ingredients became sick and died.

Eventually the alchemists realized that these metals and substances were actually dangerous poisons. Then a more correct understanding emerged. Alchemy converted from real chemistry into inner alchemy. Long-life practices began to use symbols, not substances. The philosophical ideas of wu-wei and tranquillity were combined with the spiritual practices of visualization and symbolic imagery.

The *Dragon-Tiger Classic* is one of the best-known Taoist alchemy books. Many believe it to be the oldest text on the subject, possibly written around 220 C.E. During the Sung dynasty (920–1279), the text was edited and added to the *Taoist Cannon* by two

Taoists, Wang Tao and Chou Chen-i.

The *Dragon-Tiger Classic* condenses into 1,293 words an entire system of philosophical alchemical practices that show people how to undergo a spiritual transformation. The book explains the "ingredients" and "equipment" needed, then describes what changes to expect. All ingredients, equipment, and transformations took place within the body of the practitioner. Inner cultivation through meditation replaced ingesting metals and minerals. The firing process of external alchemy was replaced with meditations that raised the fires of chi within. The ultimate enlightenment achieved by these practitioners was to experience Tao directly, from visualization and imagination.

Internal alchemists believed that the human body is One with the cosmos: the internal corresponds with the external. Taoists accepted the Tao as all-pervasive, a great Oneness from which everything emanates. Each of us is a microcosm of the great macrocosm, comprised of a mixture of yin and yang, heaven and earth. Cinnabar became a symbol within the body called the Three Fields, located in the head, heart, and an area below the navel that is called the Tan Tien—it is here that guardian spirits dwell. Demons also inhabited the body/cosmos, attacking our vitality. One way to rid the body of demons was a special purging diet that required abstaining from wine, meat, cereals, and all strong-smelling plants.

The Taoist alchemists practiced breathing techniques such as Nei Dan, embryonic breathing, and directed concentration exercises that have been incorporated into the art of chi kung (see Chapter 13). Other Taoists created special circular, slow movements that later developed into tai chi chuan (see Chapter 14), along with the use of magic talismans, magic dances, and sexual applications.

Although these practices may seem far afield from the original intent of classical Taoism, they are not. They symbolize the basic Taoist belief that life is improved when we return to Oneness with

Tao. We become One with Tao when we are quiet and tranquil, soft and flexible. Symbolic experiences help do this. We nourish our inner vitality by tapping into the deeper nature of breathing, the Primordial Breath, pulsing in synchrony with the intrinsic rhythmic cycles of Tao. The magical rituals reflect Taoist philosophy if we accept the idea that inner experience is an expression of the outer world of reality and vice versa. Then, a talisman can be viewed as an expression of Tao in the real world that can foster inner development as it fortifies Oneness.

TAOISM INTEGRATES WITH BUDDHISM AND CONFUCIANISM

The Tang dynasty gave Taoism great respect and high position and integrated Taoism into the official course of study in Chinese schools. As a result, the Taoist religion spread widely, eventually with more than fifteen hundred Taoist monasteries and many different Taoist sects throughout China.

As Taoism spread, it began to be influenced by Confucianism and Buddhism. New sects emerged, fusing these philosophies with the religious and alchemical practices already part of Taoism. The School of Complete Reality, founded by Ancestor Lu (b. 646), was a renowned Taoist sect that brought them all together.

Ancestor Lu received his early training from a traveling Taoist sage he met at an inn. Lu fell into a profound sleep and had a series of dreams in which he underwent numerous trials. He dreamt that his entire family and all his possessions were lost in a terrible fire, forcing him to emotionally let go of all his attachments. He faced ferocious wild animals and found courage. In the final trial, he turned down an enticing business arrangement that would have, in an underhanded way, made him wealthy, thus solidifying his moral character. Much like the stories told by Lieh-tzu, Ancestor Lu became enlightened through guided dreams.

The School of Complete Reality fostered the development of

three treasures—vitality, energy, and spirit—that are developed by special inner alchemical practices. Vitality must be stabilized by being pure and tranquil. The adepts were careful not to let their vitality "leak out." Energy must be guarded by developing freedom from cravings, along with openness, serenity, and self-control. Finally, the spirit is preserved by putting a stop to ruminating, letting go of emotions, and remaining empty. Buddhist concerns, such as freedom from craving and cultivation of emptiness, became primary steps along the path to Taoist enlightenment. Confucian values of purity and stability were also incorporated. The ultimate goal was to enter the Great Way, the return to Tao, only attained by nondoing. Ancestor Lu expressed these objectives in his famous statement, called "The Hundred Character Tablet":

Nurturing energy, forget words and guard it
Conquer the mind, do nondoing
In activity and quietude, know the source progenitor
There is no thing; whom else do you seek?

The trend to unify Buddhism, Taoism, and Confucianism was extended during the Sung period when people practiced Three Doctrines (*san-chiao*) together. People found that the three religions had principles that could work together, filling the gaps in any single religion.

Taoist writings were gathered into a massive collection of over fourteen hundred texts known as the *Tao Tsung* (Taoist Canon). This large body of Taoist literature was much like the Buddhist *Tripitaka*, the collection of Buddhist scriptures. Some of the Taoist texts were said to be obtained by divine revelation. The spirit of Taoism spoke through the hands of mediums, men and women who wrote in a trance, automatically. These texts were considered inspired and sacred.

TAOISM RETREATS UNDER MONGOL RULE

Genghis Khan (1155–1227) unified the Mongol tribes. They swept across China, destroying and assimilating as they rode. Genghis Khan embraced Taoism and created a Taoist patriarch as court adviser. His grandson Kublai Khan ruled all of China (1216–1294). Kublai Khan was influenced and helped by Buddhists, especially the Tibetan Lamas, one of whom created a script for writing the Mongolian language. Taoists and Buddhists debated and disputed for decades over philosophy and history at official conferences. Eventually Taoism lost favor and patronage. Taoist doctrines were incorporated into Neo-Confucianism.

PART II

Taoist Themes

Tao's unfathomable fullness
As night is part of day
The concept points beyond itself
And in its going stays
—C. Alexander Simpkins

All that we know and experience in the world comes from Tao and is a part of Tao. Taoism emphasizes certain themes and concepts, yet to truly understand Taoism, we must keep in mind that these concepts are not separate categories. Instead, they are always intertwined and interrelated. No real separation exists. When your mind is open to the Oneness of the Universe, the Taoist themes unfold for you to help you reach deeper understanding.

7
The Tao: Mystery Comes First

*At its greatest, Tao is infinite; at its smallest, there is
nothing so small but Tao is in it. That is how the myriad
things come. It is so big that it encompasses everything.
Deep like the sea, it cannot be fathomed.*

—Lao-tzu

Tao was part of Chinese philosophy for centuries, even before
Taoism and Confucianism took form. The meaning of Tao could
be pointed to but was not contained in a definition. Taoists believe
that Tao makes philosophy possible.

The Chinese, like the Indians, believed that there is an ultimate
reality which underlies and unifies the multiple things and events
we observe . . . They called this reality the Tao, which originally
meant "the Way." It is the Way, or process of the universe, the order of nature.

As time passed, the Way of Tao subdivided further. From the
One Tao, came three: the Tao of Heaven, the Tao of Earth, and
the Tao of Man. Confucianism focused on the Tao of man, or the
Way of society, emphasizing the correct, moral way to live. Taoist
philosophy became known as the Tao of Heaven, seeking the inner essence of self through the heavenly Tao. Taoism began in
mystery, based in the Tao as First Principle. The Tao is prior to
everything we know and experience; fixed codes of ethical and

moral standards are secondary. If you are faithful to Tao, morality will follow effortlessly. In this way, Taoism, which encouraged spontaneous free conduct, and Confucianism, which emphasized traditional moral conduct, can be seen not so much as competing for validity of Tao but as pointing to Tao from different directions. Eventually aspects of both philosophies combined in the Neo-Confucian movement.

TAO AS THE SOURCE

The often quoted statement of Sartre epitomizing existentialism, proclaims "Existence precedes essence." But to the Taoists, essence precedes existence. Without essence, there is no existence. Tao is the ultimate essence, the intrinsic nature from which all existence springs. For example, can you have a cup without it having a hollow space? It isn't a cup without a hollow space. The same is true for all existence. Without its essence, existence is not possible.

Tao is the source, before the created. Before life is the emptiness that is Tao. Life, or te, follows Tao. Empty space, according to Taoism is not simply nothing, it is the potential for everything. Space leaves openness to be filled. This concept is so fundamental that it is also found in Western philosophy. Plato recognized the importance of empty space:

> *Space is the mother and receptacle of all created and visible and in any way sensible things ... the universal nature which receives all bodies ... for while receiving all things she never departs at all from her own nature.*
>
> —Plato

Tao is an unchanging unity that underlies all changing phenomena. It is the unconditioned prior to conditioning. Tao is a word used to refer to the unnameable, stillness in motion, the ocean to which each in all is but a tributary stream. Tao precedes, all else succeeds. "It is bottomless, perhaps the ancestor of all things.,"

Perceptions of the world are relative because they rely on external criteria, standards that are limited by the perspective. For example, the perception of distance in space is relative to our own capacities and size. To the tiny ant, crawling to a distant mountain is too far to imagine reaching. To an eagle, the same mountain peak may seem close and reachable, a place for home.

The mushroom of a morning does not know (what takes place between) the beginning and end of a month; the short-lived cicada does not know (what takes place between) spring and autumn. These are instances of a short life. In the south of Khu there is the (tree) called Mind-ling, whose spring is 500 years and its autumn the same.

–Chuang-tzu

TAO IS USEFUL

Emptiness implies the potential for usefulness. The spokes of a wheel form around emptiness, the axle. Without it, there can be no use of the wheel: It cannot turn. The usefulness of a bowl is in its emptiness. You might fill a particular bowl to the top so that it has no further use for holding liquid, but the bowl never loses its potential to be used: Its essence as a bowl is Tao. "Tao is empty (like a bowl). It may be used but its capacity is never exhausted" (*Tao Te Ching*).

We can find the wisdom of Tao when we are silent, quiet, and flexible, making space for the Tao to appear. "Attain complete vacuity; Maintain steadfast quietude" (*Tao Te Ching*).

Return to the empty space, the core of life. Since the center is actually in the empty space, returning to nothingness restores the natural balance. In restoring the balance, we permit Tao to become manifest. Yin and yang, the natural polarity of dynamic forces, arise as the inner nature comes into being, in the Breath of Life, the chi. The Taoist, in tune with nature, must walk this path of mystery. Taoists encourage us to return to the primitive. Living closer to nature in a simple manner reveals our link to the Tao. Nature is rooted there, filled with wonderful surprises. If you are sensitive to how the Tao is expressed in self, other, and the world around you, then Taoism's path will open before you.

Tao is flexible, fluid, integrated, at one. A structure informed by Taoism would be simple, unadorned; no post or beam, no division into component parts, no separation—the center reference point is the whole itself, the unity. Each part dissolves into the whole as integral. Each part gains meaning in terms of its place within the whole.The whole also becomes a function of its parts, as the parts become a function of the whole, not separate or separable. The whole disappears as well, in the mysterious unity.

TAO AND YOU

Taoism points us back to the essentials. The essence is there all the time. We simply do not realize it when we study varied subjects, or get caught up in the demands of busy routines. But Taoism does not reject not realizing or not knowing. Not knowing can return us to the intuitive, closer to Tao. Knowing less, we will know more. Emptiness brings us closer to Tao. Knowledge is not comprehension.

> *Abandon sageliness and discard wisdom;*
> *Then the people will benefit a hundredfold.*
>
> –Tao Te Ching

Taoism offers a path to follow, to find our way back to what matters on the deepest level. Being one with Tao does not mean that you must change what you do so much as how you do it. When you center your actions in Tao, less conflict and effort results. Transformation comes from within, not from without. Be one with Tao, and everything becomes possible for you.

We do not need to know what or how.
Just be one with our nature,
Then one equals Tao
—C. Alexander Simpkins

8
Yin and Yang:
To Be Is to Be Related

Yin and yang compound together
When accepted as both true
Dissolve into a synthesis
The infinite oneness: You!
—C. Alexander Simpkins

The harmony of Tao is prior, activated by passivity, by inactivity. But as Tao is expressed in being; it generates an interchanging, dynamic play of opposites: yin and yang, the manifestation of Tao in the world. They mutually produce each other as polarities that are part of the fabric of existence.

Yin refers to characteristics of softness, passivity, femininity, darkness, the valley, and the negative, nonbeing. Yang refers to characteristics such as hardness, masculinity, brightness, the mountain, activity, being.

All active energy is manifested as these yin-yang dualities. Nonbeing accompanies being. The Tao manifests itself as change due to the flowing polar nature of energy. Energy is not static, not a fixed object. Newton's second law of motion is that for every force, there is an equal and opposite counterforce. The Taoist sage believes that every force acts with its opposite, as potential, and the opposite will act as well. Thus, if a government punishes a group severely, it may bring about its own punishment later, by that very group. The opposite, complementary force comes to be, in time, as night follows day, as winter follows summer. The Taoist sage learns to be in harmony with these cycles of activity and inactivity.

Yin and yang bring a dynamic balance of forces of movement and rest, activity and passivity, so that the balance point returns to center. The unity of opposites emerges. In many applications of Taoism, this unity is the source of guidance, the criterion, the standard by which correctness can be evaluated when reason is brought to bear on things.

Gestalt psychology formulated a general rule: The whole is greater than the sum of its parts. The tendency to form wholes, unities, predominates in perception. We see in unities, not in pieces. The Gestaltists believe that we perceive by contrast, in context. A figure is always in context to its background. A person exists in relation to the situation. We know our friends through our relationships, in terms of their lives, their backgrounds, their actions in the world. Our personal identity throughout our lives is deeply entwined with those who are meaningful to us.

YIN-YANG IN PERCEPTION

Yin and yang are built into our perceptual process. The contrast of yin and yang is absolutely essential in order for us to be able to notice things. We notice differences. There is good experimental evidence that when we are exposed to sameness, a constant or relatively unchanging stimulus over a span of time, we stop noticing it. We have all experienced this with background noise, such as the dull roar of an air conditioner or heater. At first we may be bothered by the noise, but after awhile it goes unnoticed. If we leave the room and later return, we hear the sound again. We do not tend to perceive something unless we have a difference. Sameness leads to an empty perception. We stop noticing. This same phenomenon occurs with a constant sound, a constant color in the room, or a constant smell. To be noticed, it has to make a difference. Taoism predicts this, since everything comes into being in relation to its opposite.

THE TAOIST LAW OF REVERSION

Yin and yang are so bound together that pure yin and pure yang ultimately reverse. Reversions of forces is a dynamic law of Tao, a mysterious property of the yin-yang interaction. For example, if we stare at a red square of color on a white wall, after we close our eyes, we will see the opposite color, a green square floating in the darkness. Sharp outlines of the square begin to dull, and it becomes an amorphous shape. Finally, the square loses depth and breaks up. All these reversions and others are natural responses of the retinal pigment to stimulation.

Disorder eventually reverts to order again. Even random motion, from entropy, becomes orderly. Inevitably there comes a point when randomness is evenly distributed. As soon as the extreme is reached, the situation reverts to its opposite. The extreme, the ultimate, is individual and unique to each manifestation.

Carl Rogers, founder of nondirective psychotherapy, postulated that counterbalancing the negative destructive tendency to entropy, which physicists see as a characteristic in the universe, is a positive creative tendency for order, evolution, and actualization. He called it the Formative Tendency. Taoism is optimistic about life's potential, always pointing to the intrinsic, inherent dynamics of change. This positive tendency gives us hope—hope for change, for better times.

YIN-YANG IN RELATIONSHIP—THE PATH TO INTELLIGENCE

We can intuit these elemental forces when we cultivate correct sensitivity. Following the flow of the yin-yang, we will safely navigate the oceans of life. Trust in these forces and come to terms with life's inevitable flow of vitality. Balance comes naturally, of itself. The relationship of yin and yang gives us an intelligent understanding of reality.

RECIPROCITY

In the widely accepted psychological theory of how children develop into adults, Jean Piaget proposed that mature intellectual functioning requires us to step outside our own perspective and imaginatively into another. Without this, intellectual development is stunted and limited. For the mature, sane person, our own being is not the center of the universe.

Reciprocity is fundamental understanding of reality. We include this relationship in our understandings of people, things, and events.

As children grow older, they no longer think of such expressions as "in front of" or "behind" in terms of absolutes, which indicate attributes of objects. Instead they begin to grasp the relational nature of objects in the world. A term such as "foreigner" is seen not to signify an absolute property of the person, but rather a relation which is reciprocal, so that if A is a foreigner to B, B is a foreigner to A. In a reciprocal relationship, the individual is able to see things from the other person's point of view and not only his own.

Piaget is pointing to what Taoism has long held: The mature point of view of reality is based in comprehending true relationships. Be one with the intuitive nature of things and understanding of relationship takes place of itself. Through the vision of yin and yang, relationships balance as perception embraces the other's point of view as well.

Development in life is interactive, not one way. Parents influence their children, and children in turn have an effect on their parents. Society influences its members just as its individual members can make lasting changes in society. All are in a mutual interaction in the flow.

9
Nature's Essence Revealed

Man models himself after Earth
Earth models itself after Heaven
Heaven models itself after Tao
And Tao models itself after nature
—Tao Te Ching

If the Tao is beyond names or words and cannot be seen or touched directly, how can we ever know Tao? One answer is found by studying nature.

TAO IN NATURE

The Tao expresses itself in nature. So we can be in tune with Tao when we are in tune with nature. The natural way of things unfolds spontaneously. Trees grow, flowers bloom, day passes into night. All living creatures have their instinctual way, guiding their unique character and style of living. Ducks live in lakes and ponds, swim, and dive under water. Their webbed feet and feathers are perfectly adapted to this way of life. Birds prefer to fly in the air and perch in trees. Their clawed feet and feathers are well suited to their characteristic lifestyle. All animals, from the smallest insect to the largest whale, if left to live out their lives without interference, will know how to live and what to do. Each expresses its own nature, thereby living in tune with Tao.

Human beings also have their own individual personality, a function of the Way of humanity. People can express their universal humanity by following the Tao. Tao is expressed through each of us in our particular talents and personalities. We turn away from the Tao when we try to go against our nature. Then we struggle. Modern psychology has shown that living genuinely, in accord with your true personality, feels good. Agreement between your concepts about yourself and your deepest feelings about yourself is healthy. Conflict arises from living in ways that do not feel correct for you. Sensitively attune to your inner being and allow it to lead you. Then your own life force, your vital energy, can guide you on life's path.

NATURAL LIFE CYCLE

Nature is in flux as it unfolds and grows, then shrinks and declines. All living things have their cycle from creation to destruction: they are born, they live, and they die. Within the life cycle is a continual interplay of yin and yang, activity and inactivity, tension and relaxation, being and nonbeing.

The life cycle should be allowed to evolve naturally and fully. Life becomes a struggle when people try to impose their personal will on inner nature, when they try to disrupt the natural cycles. When we learn to let things be, we live as nature intended, and orderliness and fulfilment of destiny comes of itself.

Another way to look at the cycle of life and death is being and nonbeing. Here Taoism differs from Buddhism. For the Buddhists, nothing exists, all is in flux, and anything that seems to be is merely illusion, empty due to its transitory nature. The Tao is not just the emptiness of nonbeing; it is also the fullness of being. Everything we experience in the world is part of this yin-yang cycle.

The empty space of nonbeing is a beginning. Where there is nonbeing, there is potential for Tao. Taoist sages opened themselves to Tao by quieting their minds with meditation. This applies psychologically as well. When people become rigidly filled with opinions and beliefs, there is no possibility for something new. Learn to welcome what has not yet become and you introduce a new potential for your life—Tao.

WATER

The great Tao flows everywhere. It may go left or right.
–Chuang-tzu

Look to nature to discover the ways of Tao. Water, one of nature's most life-giving substances, has been used by Taoists to symbolize Tao. Water has many special properties that make it unique. Notice the ways of water and you become aware of Tao.

When water is stirred up, it is murky, but when left undisturbed, with no currents or winds, impurities settle to the bottom. The water becomes clear, and all is perfectly reflected in the surface. When we are busy doing a lot of things, thoughts are stirred up, things become murky and unclear. Allow your mind to still and everything becomes clear. In perfect stillness we discover Tao. Chuang-tzu said, "Calm represents the nature of water at its best." Only still water reveals a reflection, never moving streams. Taoist meditations teach how to bring the mental chatter to stillness.

Water conforms to whatever shape contains it, yet water does not change its inner nature. It is always water, whether it follows a riverbed or fills a cup. Water can change its state as a liquid, to form solid ice, or even vaporize as steam, without changing its chemical nature. Similarly, Tao is formless, and yet it conforms to all things. Like water, Tao flows effortlessly, changing its expression according to circumstance, without ever giving up its inner nature. You can find ways to adapt to life's many changing situations when you flow with Tao (see Chapter 13).

Water might seem to be soft, yet the Grand Canyon is evidence of water's great power. As Lao-tzu explained:

Nothing in the world is softer than water
But we know it can wear away the hardest things. (Tao Te Ching)

Be flexible like water and you will discover indomitable perseverance, to stay with the flow of your path.

Water always tends toward the lowest places. A leak from a pipe seeps into every crevice, finding a path downward. Tao also can be found in the lowest places.

The highest excellence I liken to (that of) water.
The excellence of water appears in its benefiting all things and in its occupying, without striving (to the contrary) the low place which all men dislike. Hence (its way) is near to the Tao. (Tao Te Ching)

Science is finding that this is true. Every level of the ecosystem has an important role to play. Remove any one species and the change ripples through the entire system. Even the simplest organism may offer an organic solution to pollution—scientists have discovered and created variations of bacteria that eat petroleum wastes. From the most evolved down to the lowliest creature, each one matters in its own right, as part of the unity of nature.

Do not avoid humble, seemingly low beginnings. The noble starts low. Instead, recognize low as counterpoint to high. In embracing one side of the yin-yang you permit the other side to form. Both sides are interacting in the unity that is Tao.

This translates into daily life. Taoists advise people not to seek recognition or public acclaim. Instead, act humbly, and quietly pursue the development of personal talents. Tao is not fulfilled in external awards or recognition but in accomplishing for itself. By acting at One with the Tao, the Taoists believe that position and honors will come without effort. Thus, the Taoist does much by seeming to do nothing.

Be like water: formless yet resolute, soft yet relentless, clear and still, seeking the lowest to achieve the highest. In so doing, you find the Tao and will never be stopped.

FOLLOW NATURE

Keeping with the unspoiled and natural is the real source for healthy living. Follow the instinctual way of nature, not the external ways of people. When people become too involved in culture, a man-made fabrication, they adhere to external rules and outer controls. They lose the awareness of their intrinsic connection with the Tao through their inner nature—the instincts for what is truly the best course to take—the Tao. Turning to external controls brings about the struggles and difficulties of life. Use your intuitive inner wisdom to comprehend, and you will be attuned to Tao. The Path is clear; nothing will obstruct you.

10
Wu-Wei: To Yield Is to Conquer

Tao invariably takes no action,
And yet there is nothing left undone.
–Tao Te Ching

By taking the path of nonaction, wu-wei, nothing is left undone and everything is accomplished. On the surface this seems to be a contradiction. How can we accomplish anything without doing something to make it happen? Penetrating deeper into the meaning of nonaction offers us creative alternatives that can help make our efforts become realities.

NO ACTION CONTRARY TO NATURE

Nonaction does not mean that people should literally do nothing at all. Nonaction means to not take any action that goes against nature. Do not fight against the current; instead, flow with it and you will travel a great distance without effort. For example, lifeguards advise that if you are caught in a rip current in the ocean, always swim with the current to shore, not against its pull. If a car begins to skid on a slippery patch of road, fighting the skid by steering in the opposite direction may cause the car to whipsaw back and forth, and perhaps spin out of control. Instead, good drivers carefully and sensitively turn the wheels in the direction of the skid and take their feet off the accelerator. The car will straighten out and the driver remains in control. As the tires grip the road, the driver can once more steer without forceful effort.

The key to accomplishing is to be able to attune to the nature of what you are doing. Instead of putting effort into making something happen, become aware of what is really occurring. Look for the forces that are at work, uncover the tendencies already built into the situation. Do not fight against those forces. Use them wisely. As you ally yourself with the developing tendencies of what is about to happen, you gain control, accomplishing naturally.

Nonaction depends on a deep faith and trust in natural instincts. Drives and instincts are built in; when left to develop themselves, people tend to actualize their potential. Allow yourself to stay in tune with yourself and things work out as they are meant to.

Modern psychotherapy research has shown that learning to face and flow with whatever problems are placed in your path is more effective than fighting them. For example, positive results have been obtained when people confront phobias. Often, people try to manage their fears by avoiding the feared situation—those who fear elevators will walk up many flights of stairs rather than take an elevator, those who fear bridges will drive miles out of their way to avoid having to cross one. Modern behavioral therapy has shown that the more people avoid their fears, the worse the fears become. The accepted therapeutic technique is exposure therapy, which guides people in facing their phobias. Treatment for a fear of elevators is to ride on an elevator, carefully guided with the support of the therapist. The phobic often feels intense anxiety in doing this, but as Taoism predicts, nature takes it course. Nothing catastrophic actually happens on the elevator, and the fear eventually subsides.

The same rationale applies to the interpersonal realm. Parents often get into a power struggle with their children over homework, threatening punishment as a way of making them study. Nonaction suggests a different course: Do not take action. Search deeper into the dynamics of the situation. Does the child avoid homework for a hidden, more positive reason, as the child experiences it? For example, perhaps he or she feels a need for more play time. Contending against the outer wish rather than using the inner wish for play may cause even more difficulty, a second struggle on top of the first. Think of a more positive way to approach the objective. For example, approach homework playfully. Make a game of it. Find a way to make it fun, or work out an alternative time for play. Address the whole situation by including the inner essence with outer demands. Effective solutions are not partial solutions.

ACTION WITHOUT ACTING

Plan what is difficult where it is easy; do what is great where it is minute. The hardest things in the world begin with what is easy; the greatest things in the world begin with what is minute.
—Tao Te Ching

Taoists were early proponents of prevention. If you take action when a problem is small and easy, you will need to do much less. If, however, you wait until things become complex, the task will be much more difficult to accomplish. As the problem grows larger, the resolution takes more effort.

Imagine a logger who directs logs down the stream to the mill. If he stands at the bottom of the stream, too many logs will come at one time to direct them smoothly. All the logs will jam up together. But if the logger walks upstream, he can smoothly and easily direct each log downstream so that the flow is steady and uninterrupted.

We had an experience with fishing that illustrates this well. We were enjoying a vacation in the Caribbean islands many years ago. We had brought our fishing tackle and had set ourselves up on a promising beach with fishing poles, bait, hooks, sinkers—all the paraphernalia a modern fisherman would use. We cast our lines out and sat for a moment, then cast again and again, but nothing happened except for a powerful fish swirling. One of the islanders was watching us with a quiet smile on his face. He walked over and said in a friendly voice, "You won' catch no fish that way—only nab a shark!"

Realizing that this wise local might know something we did not, we answered, "Really? Well, how do you fish here?"

Amused, he took pity on us and said, "I show you!" With that he took a fishing line out of his pocket. He placed some bait on the hook at the end and set a colorful bobber twenty feet back. Then he swam out about a hundred feet, dropped his line, and returned to shore, tying the line to a nearby tree. "Now let's go into the restaurant out of the heat and relax!"

We accompanied him indoors and enjoyed some pleasant conversation, learning a great deal about island ways. About an hour later, we all returned to the beach and saw the bobber jumping up and down. The fish had caught itself on the hook. Our new friend casually wound up the line and brought in an enormous ten-pound fish! He said, "Now there's a nice one! I going to put one more line out and we have fish stew tonight!"

He did catch another large fish. By not doing, the fish were caught and we all took delight in the most delicious fish stew we had ever tasted.

Minimize action by doing without ado. Put the effort into the fundamental, the action itself, not the details, the frills surrounding it. Much effort is wasted on concerns surrounding the action, such as paraphernalia, appearances, getting ready, and even what other people think. Then there is less energy for the real objective and less success in the outcome.

> *He accomplishes his task, but does not claim credit for it.*
> *It is precisely because he does not claim credit that his accomplishments remain with him. (*Tao Te Ching*)*

NONACTION IN GOVERNMENT

The principle of nonaction applies to many aspects of life, but one area that interested Lao-tzu greatly was government. The only topic with more references in the *Tao Te Ching* is the Tao itself. Many of the ideas that were aimed at government policies can be readily applied to management as well as everyday life in a household.

Taoist politics could be likened to the European concept of laissez-faire: The government that governs least, governs best. Taoist sages advised rulers to stand back and let the citizens develop. As Lao-tzu said, "Ruling a great state is like cooking small fish" (*Tao Te Ching*, in Duyvendak 1992, 130). Anyone who has cooked fish knows that if you turn it too many times it will fall apart. In the same way, a government that meddles with the lives of its people will only bring about problems.

Too many complex laws and restrictions also lead to problems. Lao-tzu, Chuang-tzu, and Lieh-tzu all believed that rigid prohibitions and taboos create resistance, rebellion, and poverty. The more laws, the more thieves and robbers.

> *The more prohibitions there are, the more ritual avoidances,*
> *The poorer the people will be . . .*
> *The more laws are promulgated,*
> *The more thieves and bandits there will be.*
> *Therefore the sage has said:*
> *So long as I "do nothing" the people will of themselves be transformed. (*Tao Te Ching*)*

Lieh-tzu pointed out that a leader should be able to recognize the talents of his or her people. "In government of a state then, the hardest thing is to recognize the worth of others, not to rely upon one's own." Thus it is important for a leader to facilitate the abilities of his people and to allow them to fulfill their destinies. By removing restrictions, people will develop their talents and the whole state will benefit.

Nonaction from leaders does not mean that they are—or should be—uncaring, or that they take the leadership role lightly. Leaders must sincerely care about those being governed.

> *The weighty is the root of the light.*
> *Stillness is the lord of the restlessness ...*
> *How much less may the lord of the realm*
> *take the world lightly in his persona!*
> *By taking it lightly one loses the root.*
> *Through restlessness one loses mastery. (*Tao Te Ching*)*

Leaders should take the problems of their country and countrymen seriously, yet handle them calmly. Then they will maintain the still water of clarity as the source of wise governmental decisions.

11
Simplifying the Journey: The Way to Te

At root, then, the idea of Te is power exercised without the use of force and without undue interference with the order of surrounding circumstances.
—Alan Watts

P'U: THE UNCARVED BLOCK

Imagine for a moment that you are an accomplished woodworker. You look at an uncarved block of wood with a certain affection, knowing that here is uncreated potential. As an uncarved block it can be anything—the possibilities are infinite. No one can name it because it has not yet become something except what it is in its natural, untouched state, much like Tao.

The Taoists believe that if we could return to a state like the uncarved block of wood, *p'u*, we find Tao.

Give them Simplicity to look at, The Uncarved Block to hold.
(Tao Te Ching)

Human beings are often in a hurry to acquire the finished product, the carving. But once the item is produced, the limitless Tao is lost. A carving of an object is only that one thing. It has a name. It has come into existence. Eventually it will become worn, broken, or lost, going through its cycle of existence-nonexistence. But the original uncarved block is nameless, beyond definition, quietly open. The sage tries to be like an uncarved block, open to potential without being limited to one definition.

This idea becomes clearer by example. Many people go through a great deal of preparation for the Christmas holiday, purchasing gifts for friends and family, sending cards, and decorating their homes. The media encourages everyone to buy, inundating television, radio, and newspapers with advertisements. For some people, the preparations become so time-consuming and stressful that the inner meaning of the holiday, the Christmas spirit, often falls into the background. Taoism would point us away from the mere consumer and marketing rituals, back to the authentic nature of Christmas.

Many translators have substituted the word simplicity for p'u, the uncarved block. Simplicity is also translated as "raw silk." For the Chinese, raw silk was a material without any particular attributes, before it was dyed, sewn, or in any way shaped, much like an uncarved block of wood. Both these materials can become many things, but in their raw state, they are filled with potential. What Taoists are trying to encourage is for people to find their way back to their natural being before it is influenced and shaped by culture. There is a simple, pure nature in all of us, and this nature is One with Tao. Through society we learn to be limited. We experience restraints, norms, and have many experiences that shape us. We form arbitrary and relative definitions of ourselves, alienated from our inborn nature.

Like the Taoist sage, hypnotherapist Milton Erickson believed that our unconscious mind is the true self. As we travel through life, we learn to have limits. Negative experiences from teachers, parents, and society all seem to communicate "You cannot do this. That is impossible." Problems arise from these learned limitations.

Erickson taught people to return to their unconscious mind, using trance. Then they would resolve conflicts or let go of them. The natural flow of unconscious functioning helps resolve things effortlessly. In trance, you do not have to do anything in particular except allow nature to take its course (see Part III). Return to the uncarved block and you will be who you truly are, one with your original nature, one with Tao.

THE POWER OF P'U

It is life near the bone where it is sweetest.
–Henry David Thoreau

Tao is the source, Te follows. Te of Taoism comes from remaining in the mental state of p'u, the uncarved block. By letting be, facilitating others, lead by permitting, standing back to be ahead, potential to influence begins to happen. Thus the ruler (who may be interpreted as the head of a business or the head of a household—a good parent) knows that there are times to step back and allow the employee, the child, to develop and grow. Then, others do not experience the leader as an obstruction because they are not impeded. Be below to be above. The sage desires little, wants not to want, seeks not what the multitudes seek in order to regulate the flow of events.

Te is in Tao. Inner nature, intuitively followed as a guide, leads to Tao, for it is in tune with the lawful nature of the universe. Accept the good and the bad as well, the kind and the cruel in nature. The rainstorm and the sunny day both have their beauty and virtue. The sage remains calm in the center.

DISCOVERING TE B Y FOLLOWING THE WAY

To thine own self be true,
And it must follow, as the night the day
Thou can't not then be false to any man.

–Shakespeare, *Hamlet*

Te is the living expression of Tao in us all as we live our lives. There are many interpretations of Te's exact meaning: power, virtue, life itself. All of these reflect that Te means life and the conduct of living, power and its influence in life. The very name of the book, *Tao Te Ching*, shows us how Tao must inevitably be followed by Te. The two are linked, as Tao finds expression in life.

The entire second half of the *Tao Te Ching* articulates guidelines for life and conduct of living. All of these embody Te. Cherish life, Lao-tzu teaches. Life is nourished by Tao. The practices of spiritual alchemy, meditation, and exercises for health and longevity that characterize Taoism today offer practical methods.

Te can be understood more easily when we look at how differently it is applied in Confucianism from Taoism. Confucianism employs the words "Tao" and "Te" but uses them in a manner opposite to Taoism. For Confucians, the human being, culture, and civilization and its rituals are the source for the guidelines of life. Taoists believe the source for life's guidelines is always found in Tao. Personal conduct, family, culture, and civilization follow Tao.

Understanding how to act comes from the person in relationship to Tao rather than from rules, organizations, or even culture imposed from outside. Guidelines for action are not defined by external concepts but are found within. Thus Taoism is an internally based theory, with empathy and sensitivity to the flow as the central principle for relating to others.

If we seek to guide our actions only by an external standard, a criterion outside the situation we are part of, we fail. External standards must be individualized to apply. Start by looking at your own personal situation first. From this, contemplate the Tao of situations in general to find inspiration for guidance. Individual situations are a living expression of the greater Tao.

Whomsoever moulds his person, his life becomes true.
Whomsoever moulds his family, his life becomes complete.
Whomsoever moulds his community, his life will grow.
*Whomsoever moulds the world, his life will become broad. (*Tao Te Ching*)*

Live according to Tao and life's choices will not confuse you. Return to the origins to know the ending. The uncarved block leads to wisdom. The Tao is in each as in all, and thus one can extend one's life and capacities through the family, the community, the country, and, ultimately, the world. To return to the true self, help others and the family to recognize and live in Tao. Great wisdom and good judgment can thereby be found and expressed. Judge each within its own group or class, not against individuals.

For example, Lao-tzu believes that to understand families, begin with your own. The individual family, if comprehended in its deepest sense, leads naturally to the understanding of families in general. Start where you are, not from an external ideal. Each thing expresses Tao and therefore, can lead to its individual Tao, and then to the universal Tao itself. The true essence is the higher reality within things.

This point is illustrated by a patient of Dr. John Whitehorn, who was chief of staff at Johns Hopkins University Hospital, Phipps Clinic psychiatric ward. When Whitehorn was doing his residency in psychiatry, he met a schizophrenic patient who was very sensitive and rejected all attempts to reassure away her extreme discomfort in her family. She explained the reason why she was refusing to cooperate with the treatment: "You don't know my aunt Sophia!" At first Dr. Whitehorn was puzzled, but eventually he met her aunt Sophia. After talking with her, he realized the patient's concerns were well-grounded in reality. Her aunt Sophia was a demanding, powerful, autocratic person, very difficult to get along with. He told his patient, "Yes. I understand. I met her. I do know your aunt Sophia." This became the basis for rapport and a subsequent positive therapeutic relationship that helped the patient to heal. We all have an aunt Sophia in our lives—not just people, but circumstances that are unique and intimately related to meaning and values. Only through becoming one with our situation can we know what to do, and when we do, our intuition guides us well. Empathy follows here as well, so that we may help others. What is your aunt Sophia like?

DESIRING LESS

How do we express Te in our lives? One pathway is to give up the desire for excess. Then life becomes simpler, not complicated by more than is needed. The Taoist view concerning excessive desire is not quite the same as the Buddhists, to whom craving in general is the root of all problems. Taoists believe we should let go of culturally based extremes and unnatural desires such as the wish to accumulate possessions or the drive for power. By the principle of yin-yang, the opposite is always created. Owning too much creates a potential for its opposite. A string of inevitable problems emerges, such as maintaining these belongings and, ultimately, worrying about losing them. Objects of value in themselves breed thieves, according to the *Tao Te Ching*, since it is only natural that others will want for themselves those objects that are given value by the culture. "No lure is greater than to possess what others want" (*Tao Te Ching*).

The value of an object is relative, often culturally determined, not intrinsic to the object itself. For example, people often wish to own more and more computer software even though it can be very costly. It has become so highly sought after that software pirates have come into being, illegally copying and selling it. But an aborigine who has never seen a computer might think that a computer software disk is a worthless piece of plastic and throw it away. To a four-year-old, CD disks are just toys.

Stop placing a higher value on outer things. Return to the intuitive wealth within: the Tao. Then you will be happy, tranquil, and develop your Te naturally:

Reveal thy simple self
Embrace thy original nature,
Check thy selfishness
*Curtail thy desires. (*Tao Te Ching*)*

The drive to take control and power for their own sake leads people away from Tao. Whenever we try to take control of a person or a circumstance, the opposite is created. Resistance and conflict fill the situation, bringing progress to a halt. Give up attempts to take control. Then the true dynamics are revealed and can be guided in positive directions. Helpful facilitation is much more powerful and lasting than domination. When we are One with Tao, we have greater insight and more developed abilities.

This story from Lieh-tzu illustrates: Once there was a man who had great affection for seagulls. He liked to take a swim each morning among them. The seagulls flocked to him, perched on him, almost as if he was one of them. One day his father said, "You seem to have a way with those birds. Catch one for me and I will make it my pet."

Being an obedient son, he agreed. The next day, when he went out to swim with the gulls, they flew around high above his head but would not perch. It was as if they had somehow been alerted. The change in the young man's mind had communicated his intent to take control over the birds. He was no longer One with them, and their natural instincts told them to stay away. Animals can sense intent and respond appropriately.

TRANQUILLITY

Taoist philosophy can be experienced in tranquillity. Calm your mind, turn attention away from the outer world, and allow your thoughts to become clear like water. This is the pathway to enlightenment. Feel the ripples, notice nuances and subtlety. Take pleasure in the simple things. Do not let mental life become completely filled. Leave open spaces, time to simply contemplate quietly without any particular data in mind. To be free to grow fully and develop yourself, don't be busy all the time! This is true wealth.

THE BENEVOLENCE OF TE

> *The more he does for others The more he possesses.*
> *The more he gives to others The more he has.*
>
> –Tao Te Ching

Te is a subtle power, intended as a benevolent one. Lao-tzu, Chuang-tzu, and Lieh-tzu offer much ethical advice on how people should live their lives. They intended that sages would help others as part of their nonacting, tranquil way of life. People should be kind to others. Be good to the good people and also to those not so good, be faithful to the positive in all, for life is faithfulness. The Taoist sage communicates these values quietly by honoring Tao and cherishing life, in tune with the music of the universe.

The sage guides culture in a peaceful, benevolent direction, and everyone fulfills their natural potential. When people stop seeking selfish ends and cease feeling overly greedy for gain, they no longer seek power and dominance over others. Conflicts and problems diminish of themselves. By letting be, events evolve according to their natural cycles. Life force circulates and all works out for the best. Hot, bitter aggression boils away, leaving a cool, sweet, peaceful world.

PART III
Living Taoism

All things are held in yin, and carry yang:
And they are held together in the chi of teeming energy.
–Tao Te Ching

As Tao comes into being, the polar opposites yin and yang arise. Chi is the breath of life. The early classical Taoists turned to immersion in the experience of Tao itself, becoming tranquil and quiet, forgetful of all else. Later Taoists sought to express Tao in chi, since chi arises from Tao, thereby extending Tao into our world. There are many areas where Taoism has found application in everyday life. Participants begin with a calm, tranquil center in the experience of Tao, then express Tao in motion, in life, as chi directed outwards. Meditation, Chi Kung, Eastern medicine, martial arts, art, and psychotherapy offer ways to apply these principles for a healthier, happier, more energetic life, at One with Tao.

12
Meditation:
Deep Calm, Vital Energy

Attaining the utmost vacuity and earnestly observing
quietness, while the ten thousand things all together are
operating, I contemplate their return (to nothingness).
—Tao Te Ching

Deep within the sea of consciousness we search for Tao. Meditation helps us navigate through the waters. Following the flowing circulation of chi as our compass, in tune with Tao, we can explore more deeply. Meditation can bring about clarity of thoughts, calming, along with greater vitality, sensitivity, flexibility, and resiliency. Taoists believe that the practice of meditation brings about healthier and happier living. Many traditional Taoist meditations are included in the next two chapters, along with modern adaptations to help you find your Way to Tao.

CALMING

Since Lao-tzu, Taoists have advocated quieting the mind. Although the early classical Taoists did not offer step-by-step instructions, they refer to meditation as holding the key to becoming receptive. Later Taoist movements formulated varied meditations for people to follow. This series of exercises will help you develop inner calm and clear perceptions the Taoist way, so that it seems to be happening without effort.

If you have any difficulty doing a meditation, take a break. Get up, walk around, and then try again. Or try again later, in bed before you fall asleep or when you first wake up in the morning. Remember that naturalness is central for Taoist meditation.

CALMING THE BODY

Mind and body are linked. One pathway to a tranquil mind is through the body. You can relax without forcing it by applying certain methods of meditation.

ALLOWING BODY RELAXATION

Find a place to meditate where you will not be distracted. Lie on the floor on your back with your arms resting at your sides. Raise your knees so that your feet are resting flat on the floor. Take a few moments and lie quietly. Let your attention wander to your body; notice where you are tight and where you are relaxed. Are you tensing any muscles? Notice how your body meets the floor. Are you pushing against it or are you allowing your muscles to let go to the floor, almost as if you are sinking or floating? At first, do not try to change anything. Simply notice what you feel and wait.

After several minutes your muscles may release excess tension. Wait for your body to respond on its own. Do not do anything except be open to the possibility that you could be more relaxed. People who carry excess muscle tension sometimes become so accustomed to it that they do not allow the possibility of change. Allow your muscles to be as relaxed as they want to be, but do not force relaxation. Be attentive to the feeling of willingness in your muscles. Increase the time spent in this meditation as much as is comfortable. Repeat this exercise at other times.

CALMING THINKING

Relaxing the body can bring about a quieting of the mind—as

you may have experienced in the previous exercise. Inner calm can also be developed through mental exercises.

Tao always expresses itself as opposites. Thus stillness does not have to mean absence of movement or passivity. It could manifest itself as stilling undesirable tendencies, such as impatience or thoughtless outbursts. A calm mind can manifest itself in many areas of life. You just need to discover your own natural balance between quiet and activity.

For this meditation, find a quiet room. Pick a time when you know you will not be disturbed for at least five minutes. If you would like to follow the classical tradition, sit on a small cushion on the floor. Some people find it difficult to sit on the floor; if so, find a comfortable chair. The mental state is what is important for these meditations, not the physical position.

Sit quietly for a minute or two. Do not think about anything in particular. Notice any thoughts or images that occur to you but try not to get lost in any one thought. Bring yourself back to the present moment and simply sit quietly. As with the body meditation above, do not force anything. Let your mind find its natural rhythm for thoughts. If they are racing, wait for them to slow down a little. If your mind feels blank, ask whether you could have a few ideas. Encourage your thoughts to find the correct balance, like a buoy righting itself in water. Wait quietly. In time you will find that your mind becomes calm naturally.

POSITIVE FORGETFULNESS

Our thoughts reach out to the world around us. We think about our plans, our wishes, our worries. Taoist hermits sought internal calm by stepping away from the external world. They often lived in seclusion, close to nature. They drew on their experiences whenever they encountered everyday society. Sages guided people to take a break from the pressures without having to go anywhere.

"Without leaving his door; He knows everything under heaven" (Tao Te Ching).

Close your eyes as you sit in a quiet, comfortable place, away from any disturbances. Imagine that you are going on a journey. It could be a place you have actually visited and enjoyed or a vacation you would like to take. Pick a spot that is quiet and peaceful, preferably close to nature. As you begin to imagine yourself there, feel all the concerns of home slipping away. You do not lack for anything or desire anything. You have plenty of time to relax and enjoy the beauty around you—simply delight in the experience. Maintain the image for several minutes. Return to this calm, desireless state of mind whenever you need a break.

CLEAR MIND: MIRROR MEDITATION

By cleansing your secret mirror, can you make it without blemish?
—Tao Te Ching

When you make your mind as still as a lake on a windless day, you can see everything reflected. Then you will be able to recognize what you need to do and how to go about it: everything becomes clear. With mental calm comes increased acuity. Your world is illuminated for you. Your perceptions clarify.

In Taoist literature, mirrors took on a special significance. "When lit by the sun, the fires of heaven appear." If the moon is reflected, it shows the heavenly dew. Mirrors can make visible what is missed by normal perception. You can enhance the clarity of your own perceptions with this ancient meditation.

Close your eyes. Imagine a vast brightness that becomes brighter and brighter until it transforms into a mirror reflecting all over your body, as if you have become a mirror. Let yourself experience the clarity of the mirror. What do you see reflected? Try not to interfere with any thoughts about it. Simply experience what is there for you.

KEEPING THE ONE

He who knows the One has accomplished everything
He who knows the One knows all …
The Tao reveals itself first of all in the One
It is therefore of incomparable value.

–Kristofer Schipper

Keeping the One is a Taoist practice that brings you closer to Tao. When you keep the One, you find balance in your life among mind, body, and spirit.

We have all, at times, experienced the One, if only for a brief moment; that feeling when everything is flowing smoothly and we are in harmony with our thoughts, feelings, and the environment. The more difficult challenge is to maintain this experience when circumstances push and pull away from balance. Keeping the One in these situations takes skills that you can develop with meditation.

The spiritual dimension is always in harmony with everyday life, yet at the same time in tune with nature. But how do we go about doing this? It requires openness and receptivity of mind. The following exercises help develop skills.

START WITH THE SMALL

The journey of a thousand miles begins with one step. Begin with something small and everything follows. Henry David Thoreau found great pleasure in observing the subtlest details of nature.

During his Walden Pond experiment, he spent many hours lost in his observations. Most of us do not have the time that Thoreau devoted to contemplating nature. Although he gives a good argument for making the time, we can take the same open attitude and enjoy a small moment with just as much intensity. He described his experience:

> *I sat in my sunny doorway from sunrise till noon, rapt in a revere amidst the pines and hickories and sumacs, in undisturbed solitude and stillness, while the birds sang around or flitted noiseless through the house. . . . I grew in those seasons like corn in the night. (Henry David Thoreau)*

Go outside and find some small thing in nature to observe. It could be a flower, a small insect, a bird, or even a bit of sand or a blade of grass. Sit before it and observe carefully. Notice everything about it. If it is grass, does it move with the wind? Notice the colors of the flowers, the delicacy of the petals. Observe the bird, how it moves, what sounds it makes—its bird nature in action. Let yourself become fascinated with it. Allow yourself to feel what you feel about it. Bring all your emotions and thoughts together in this single moment of experience of nature.

KEEPING THE ONE IN ACTIVITY

After you feel that you have been successful with the previous exercise, try extending this open, natural attitude into something you do regularly. For example, try it when working in the yard. Before you begin, calm your mind. Rather than following a predetermined plan, let your natural inclinations, inspired by the garden itself, guide you in where to begin. Then let yourself begin to work. Lose yourself in sweeping or raking. Follow the contours of the ground with your strokes. If clipping, try to stay attuned to the plant and what it seems to need. You will know when you are ready to stop. Do not push beyond this if things are left undone, but return another time when you feel ready.

VISUALIZATION

Taoist meditations work with visualization. Taoist sects used many forms of visualization to help foster inner transformation. Symbolic imagery is a contemporary therapeutic tool that helps reach into areas where the conscious mind may not succeed. If you have difficulty visualizing, please refer to our book *Principles of Meditation* where we have given step-by-step instructions on how to visualize.

There is an unconscious link between mind and body. We rely on it throughout the day without conscious direction. What we imagine in our minds often becomes reality without any conscious effort. To experience this for yourself, think about a tart lemon. Vividly try to picture it in your mind. Most people will feel an increase of salivation in their mouth. This automatic mechanism of mind, called the ideomotor effect, was activated by Taoists in some of their visualization meditations. The following meditations use your imagination to help bring about positive experiences.

Visualization Meditation 1: Red Breath

Sit upright so that your breathing passages are clear—you can also do this standing. As you inhale gently, imagine that the air you are inhaling is red. Exhale the red air gently. Imagine that the red air is like a warm fire within, and it becomes brighter and warmer as you breathe, moving from your center out to your extremities, filling you with warm, vibrant energy. Keep your attention on your breathing, visualizing the red air flowing through you.

Visualization Meditations 2: Sun's Light

The Taoists believe that we can enhance our internal energy by becoming One with the energy around us from the sun, associated with yang, and the moon, associated with yin. For both of these meditations, you may wish to recall memories of the sun and the moon, or perhaps create new images.

Sit quietly and breathe comfortably. Imagine that the sun shines down on you. Feel the sunlight on your skin as a slight warmth; then, gradually, the light penetrates through you, so that you feel yourself aglow with the bright warm light of the sun. Imagine that you soak in the energy, that the sun's rays stimulate your inner energy to flow freely and unobstructed. You might begin to feel some tingling sensations or warmth develop in your hands or feet. If so, let the feeling spread. Remain relaxed as you imagine sunbathing.

Visualization 3: Moon's Luminescence

At another time, sit quietly and breathe comfortably as before. This time, imagine a full moon above. As you sit, the gentle radiance of the moon sends a glow onto your skin. Let the luminescence penetrate through you, so that you feel yourself glowing with the soft, silvery light. Notice the sensations you feel from this. Let your energy flow freely within as you remain relaxed, contemplating the moon. Enjoy the experience of moonbathing.

13
Chi Kung: Enhance Well-Being

"By concentrating your breath until you become soft,
can you be like an infant?"
–Tao Te Ching

FLEXIBILITY IN DOING

The Way of water is formless, flexible, adaptable, relentless, unstoppable. Water flows, yet it stays: Its nature does not change. Water can take on the shape of whatever container it is in. When introduced to another vessel, with a new shape, it takes on that new shape. Actions that are rigid, held to regardless of circumstance, are bound to failure: Even if there is temporary success, the rigidity is not positive.

Learning to be more flexible generally can become a possible response to life situations. Taoist techniques help to enhance suppleness of the body and increase the flow of chi. These methods are a natural outgrowth of the philosophy. To flow like water, your body must become flexible. The following exercises help you discover your own flexible response.

FLEXIBILE BODY

Taoist yin-yang theory suggests that whenever we push in one direction, a tendency to go in the opposite direction is also created. This has been shown to be true in modern theories of stretching and flexibility. The American Academy of Orthopaedic Surgeons defines flexibility as the range of motion at a specific joint, that is the capacity to lengthen or stretch. To become more flexible as Taoism advises can be enhanced by a physical program to help elongate the muscles. But how you stretch can have the opposite effect if you do not do it correctly.

STRETCHING PRINCIPLES

Most people are familiar with the static stretch, a slow, gentle stretch. In this approach, the muscle tissue is stretched to a comfortable position and held for a period of time. Bouncing or sudden forcing has been shown not to work. The body reacts to a sudden bounce by tightening up more. Breathe gently. Stretch slowly. When you take the time to ease into a stretch you can become aware of your muscles and gradually extend your capacities for flexibility.

Approach all of these flexibility exercises slowly, without forcing the movements. Back off if you feel pain. Allow your meditative mind to stay in tune with your body by focusing all your attention on the movements. Let your muscles be rounded when performing the exercises. Permit your muscles and joints to remain as soft and relaxed as possible, without becoming slack.

Slow, relaxed, continuous movements enhance flexibility. Let your motions be natural, soft, and flowing. This general approach can lead not only to looser muscles but also to a healthier body. These stretches incorporate this way of moving for stretching. Wear loose-fitting, comfortable clothes.

Neck Loosening

Stand with legs shoulder width apart and hands on your hips. Close your eyes. Slowly turn your head to the right, then around to the left. Repeat several times. Next, tilt your head back, and then tip your chin toward your chest. Repeat this pattern. Do not push—keep the motion smooth and slow. Breathe comfortably. Focus all your attention on your neck. If you notice any tightness as you rotate, let it go.

Shoulder Relaxation

Let your hands hang down beside your legs. Raise your shoulders very slowly toward your ears until they are as high as you feel comfortable holding them. Then, slowly and smoothly lower them until they are completely relaxed. Keep your attention focused on the motion. Repeat this two or three times, pausing at the top before you lower them again. When you have reached the bottom, pause to allow as much relaxation as possible. Like the exercise above, perform the movements slowly with relaxed breathing. Next, rotate your shoulders in a circle, forward, then backward. If you notice tension as you move, see if you can let go of the excess tightness.

Tai Chi Chuan Body Swings

This exercise applies the same kind of motions to your entire body. Stand with your legs shoulder width apart and your arms at your side. You may do this exercise with your eyes closed. Slowly and gently twist your body around to the left, allowing your feet to pivot. Lightly and gently swing your relaxed arms with the turn. Without stopping, swing loosely around to the right. Do not force or do extreme motions. Keep your breathing relaxed and your mind focused on the experience. Try to let your body move in unison, from head to toe in smooth, slow, flowing motions.

You can apply this principle of slow, relaxed continuous movement to other loosening exercises. Relax and slow down. Breathe comfortably and maintain awareness of your movements.

FLEXIBLE MIND

Taoists encourage flexibility. Flexibility of body is one part, but equally important is flexibility of mind. Flexible mind can help you find new solutions to problems and flow with circumstance. It is primary in creativity, opening new ways to see things. The following exercises will help you experiment with mental flexibility.

Figure-Ground Meditation

Look at the figure below. It is called the Necker Cube, first described by the Swiss crystallographer L. A. Necker in 1832. The cube can be seen from two perspectives. When you perceive the second perspective the figure seems to jump into the new projection, where the front appears to move to the back and the top seems to move to the bottom. Relax your mind for a few moments. Then look at the figure. Watch it until it shifts. If you do not see

Necker Cube

it change, look away and then look back again. Practice shifting your perspective until you can make it shift naturally, back and forth. Let your perception be flexible.

Yin-Yang Meditation

This exercise involves creative perception with yin and yang. Sit comfortably and close your eyes for a brief meditation. Let your mind relax for a few minutes (see Chapter 12). Once you feel relaxed, picture the color red. Think about it. If you can, visualize the color. Think of an object that is red. After a few minutes, think of the opposite on the color circle: green. Visualize this just as you did with red. Imagine that the object you were picturing turns green. Shift back and forth between the two colors.

Experiment with other opposite pairs. Let yourself come up with creative possibilities. Try thinking of a situation in your life and then imagine that it is the opposite. Shift back and forth, playfully and flexibly.

RAISING VITALITY WITH CHI KUNG

Chi kung is the meditative art that circulates internal energy, chi. Derived from Taoism, chi kung has been combined with martial arts and Eastern medicine to enhance health, strength, and vitality. Chi kung practice raises chi at will, to circulate and direct it to various parts of the body. Martial artists can use it to add to the effectiveness of their blocks and strikes. Applied for health, chi kung helps to unblock stagnant chi, returning the body to its correct balance of yin and yang by the healthy circulation of energy.

Chi kung has many exercises to help enhance vitality. Chi is generated locally and circulated for health, well-being, and strength. You can perform chi kung either moving or still. Nei dan is performed while sitting. Moving chi kung, is known as wai dan. Experiment with both forms on a regualr basis.

When you perform any kind of chi kung, keep your muscles toned yet rounded, soft, and relaxed. The flexibility exercises above have prepared you to keep relaxed without being slack. Various systems exist, both traditional and modern innovations.

NEI DAN: SITTING MEDITATION

Nei dan, the method of meditation that was first developed as part of the Taoist sects, works with breathing to help raise chi and circulate it from a seated position. Translated as "internal elixir," nei dan traditionally generated chi from a point one and a half inches below the navel in the part of the abdomen called the tan tien. Taoist alchemists thought of this area as a metaphor for the furnace where the metals were melted together. Similarly, our internal energy is fired up by concentrating attention on the tan tien. Once chi is raised, this area around the abdomen becomes warm with energy. Further meditation directs chi to circulate throughout the body. Relax before you begin each session by performing a calming meditation from Chapter 12.

Breathing Down to Your Heels

Taoism fosters living naturally and relaxed. What better place to begin than the very fundamental activity in which we all engage throughout life: breathing. Chuang-tzu spoke of breathing that circulated energy through the whole body when he said, "The men of old breathed clear down to their heels." When you develop whole body breathing, your vitality is raised.

Sit comfortably straight, so that your air passages are clear. Inhale through your nose and let the air move all the way down into your lungs. Let your lungs fill fully and your rib cage and stomach expand as the air moves all the way down into the tan tien region. Exhale slowly, beginning with the lower abdomen; gently push the air up and out through your nose. Breathe in again and let your lungs and abdomen expand. Breathe out as you gently contract your stomach. Let your breathing be slow, continuous, and gentle. Do not force it or hyperventilate. Begin with short breaths and gradually lengthen them as you become more accustomed to doing this.

As you breathe fully, imagine that with every inhalation you bring energy and vitality into your body. With each exhalation you let out impurities. Some of the traditional Taoist meditations used an image of colored light coming in and darkness leaving.

When you become comfortable with this meditation your

breathing becomes effortless. Eventually you will feel as if your whole body breathes, even down to your heels.

Embryonic Breathing: Raising Chi in the Tan Tien

Taoists point out that, in the womb, the fetus breathes through the umbilical cord, attached through the abdomen. This breathing is the opposite of natural breathing, in which we expand our abdomen when we breath in and deflate it when we exhale. Watch a very young infant and you will see the opposite happen: The stomach expands as the child exhales. Taoists believe that we can regain our original tranquillity and reclaim the vital energy we had as infants by performing embryonic breathing.

As you inhale, do not expand your abdomen. Instead, let your abdomen gently contract as your chest expands. Then, in a continuous flow, exhale, allowing your chest to flatten while your abdomen expands. Breathe lightly and push very gently. Keep your attention directed on the air as it flows in and out. Work on developing a continuous flow and gradually lengthening your breaths. The tan tien area becomes warm as you raise your chi in this area.

Circulating Your Chi

Vividly imagine that you are holding a large beach ball of energy in your lap. Rest your arms on top of the ball so that your hands are raised and your arms are comfortably bent outwards at the elbows in a semicircle held slightly away from you. Permit the energy to move out from your tan tien, around through your arms and hands. The energy ball may expand slightly as the energy circulates for several minutes. Extend the time as you like.

For a variation, imagine rolling the energy ball from side to side, letting your hands rotate around it. Twist gently as you roll the ball to your left, allowing your left hand to move to the top as the right hand moves to the bottom. Then roll the ball to the right. Let the ball roll freely.

Directing Your Chi

Perform one of the breathing exercises above. Once you are feeling the warmth and tingling of energy, direct your attention to your hands. Concentrate all your attention there and imagine the energy streaming to your hands. You can create a vivid picture or imagine it as a stream of sensations. Keep your attention on your hands. Practice helps you to feel the tingling and warmth move to your hands. You can experiment with circulating the energy to areas where you are tight or sore, such as your shoulders or neck, or move the energy into an injury or discomfort you might have. This can work well to enhance any medical treatment you are already undergoing. (See Chapter 14 for further development of this exercise.)

WAI DAN: MOVING MEDITATION

Wai dan can help you feel the link between mental concentration and energy flow to the muscles. Movements are done slowly, without tension, to promote free circulation of chi. Wai dan has a number of formal, traditional series of movements. One of the better-known forms is called the Eight Pieces of Brocade. Another is the Muscle Change Exercise, created by Bodhidharma for the monks at the Shaolin temple and described in the *I Chin Ching* (the Muscle Change Classic).

Here is a simpler introductory group of wai dan exercises. As you perform each one, keep your mind focused on the area you are moving. Move slowly; notice the sensations as you move. When done correctly, you will feel relaxed and revitalized after a session. Your energy level may increase overall.

Relaxed Standing

Before you begin any moving chi kung patterns, stand quietly for a few moments. Let your posture be natural, with feet approximately shoulder width apart, arms hanging down at your sides, hands open. Close your eyes and bring your thoughts to the present moment. Notice sensations of standing: how your feet meet the ground, how the air feels on your skin, and anything else you can feel. Keep your balance centered evenly between your feet. When you feel you have focused your attention and gathered yourself fully, open your eyes to begin.

Pattern 1: Touching Heaven and Earth

Stand with your legs shoulder width apart. Bring your hands up to around shoulder height, with palms facing forward. Focus your attention on body sensations. Let your posture be naturally balanced, upright, and without strain. Slowly extend your left hand above your head with your palm facing up toward the sky. At the same time, gently extend your right hand downward in front of you, palm facing the ground. Inhale smoothly as you push gently in both directions simultaneously. Reverse the position of your hands so that your left hand pushes down and your right hand pushes up. Exhale with this movement. Remain relaxed; breathe comfortably with all your attention concentrated on the movements. Breathe naturally, without changing the volume or intensity of your breaths. Do not exaggerate your breathing. Repeat the pattern ten times.

Pattern 2: Issuing from the Roots

Stand with your legs a little wider than shoulder width apart. In martial arts, this is called the horse stance because your legs are positioned as if you are riding a horse. Begin by bending your knees slightly as you bring your hands to rest gently on your thighs and inhale gently. Keep your back relatively straight. Bend your knees only as far as is comfortable. Keep your weight evenly balanced over your legs. Straighten your legs without locking them and exhale. Keep your attention focused on the motion in your legs. Repeat ten times.

This time as you bend, shift your weight over the left leg. Your right leg will not bend very much. Inhale as you bend and remain relaxed. Return to an evenly balanced standing position as you exhale. Next, as you bend your knees, shift your weight over your right leg. Inhale and relax. Exhale as you straighten and return to your evenly balanced upright position. Repeat ten times, alternating between left and right.

Pattern 3: Circling with Tao

Take the horse stance, as in the previous exercise. Make a large, slow, circling motion with your left hand, moving across your body with your palm up and then up over your head turning your palm down. We often tell students when we are teaching this exercise to imagine that you are scooping up water and then dropping it on your head. Let your whole body flow with the motion from your feet on up. Your legs will bend naturally, as in the previous exercise, as you move your arm around. Breathe slowly, in and out as you circle. Try to remain relaxed as you move. After ten circles, switch to the right hand and repeat the pattern.

Pattern 4: Flowing with the Universe

This pattern combines hands and feet. Begin by standing with your feet shoulder width apart and your hands open at your waist, elbows bent. Step forward with your left leg, bending your knee slightly and letting your weight move over the front leg. At the same time, extend both hands forward, palms forward, as if you are pushing a large object away from you. Inhale gently. Coordinate the movement so that your hands and foot move together, slowly and without tension. Bring your foot back to the starting position as you simultaneously bring your hands back to your waist. Exhale as you move. Repeat the same pattern with your right foot. Perform these movements ten times, alternating between right and left foot.

After you are finished, you might feel some tingling or warmth in the areas you have moved. This is the sensation of your chi. These exercises raise vitality and let it flow, unblocked, through your entire body.

14

Healing: Finding Harmony

Since the human body is part of the world of nature—indeed, is a natural microcosm in itself—it is subject to the same laws that govern the universe.

—Katsusuke Serizawa

Eastern medicine is a sophisticated and highly evolved approach to healing that has become a multibillion-dollar part of our health-care system. Chronic pain and many physical conditions can be worked with and in many cases helped by Eastern medicine. Standard Western medical practice can also be extended and supplemented using Eastern methods. By including Eastern medicine in Western practice, new options become available for treatment. Many American and European medical and dental schools now include alternative medicine courses to familiarize doctors with it. In France, a medical doctor has the option to specialize in acupuncture. In the United States, more and more people are turning to acupuncture for treatment.

Western doctors usually treat patients only when they get sick. Like the old saying "If it ain't broke, don't fix it," the Western doctor does not presume to intervene or intrude into a patient's lifestyle. Doctors of Oriental medicine, however, take a preventive approach. Traditionally, Chinese doctors were given the task of keeping people healthy. They were judged by their ability to prevent illness and were paid when the villagers stayed healthy, not when they got sick. A yearly checkup anticipated and prevented illnesses that could be problematic later. Modern practitioners must use a different system of payment, of course, but still point treatment toward optimal functioning.

TAOISM IN EASTERN HEALING

Eastern medicine is based on the Taoist theory of unity. The harmonious interactive unity of organisms living in their environment is healthy, being One with Tao. Illness is a symptom of disturbance in the harmonious balance of the body system. Healing involves restoring a healthy, dynamic equilibrium. Any disharmony within the body ripples throughout to affect the whole.

Healthy functioning depends on circulation of chi through the veinlike channels known as meridians. These are not veins but paths that the trained and sensitive practitioner has studied and can locate. Proper stimulation of key points along the meridian system can unblock, intensify, or reroute chi to promote healing. Each meridian has a function. Some meridians are yang and others are yin. All are part of the cyclic flow of vitality throughout the body. Yin and yang balance are part of the diagnosis of difficulty. A balance is found by using acupuncture, acupressure, massage, chi kung, and herbs, often in combination. These different pathways to treatment exist in a complex interrelationship.

Acupuncture originally developed as one of the healing arts in Taoism. Eventually, though, Eastern medical practices such as acupuncture grew away from Taoism and became their own separate discipline. Acupressure is another form of Chinese medicine; it uses the same theory as acupuncture but relies on noninvasive pressure with fingertips instead of needle insertion. Herbs also affect yin-yang balance, enhancing chi.

WHAT EASTERN MEDICINE TREATS

Eastern medicine can be very helpful with conditions affected by psychological processes such as ulcers, acne, migraines, and muscle spasms. It is also very effective for problems Western medicine cannot treat. When your body hurts and your doctor says, "We can't find anything specifically wrong; there's not much you can do about it but rest," or even, "You'll just have to live with it; this is very common, and many people have it worse," it may be time to consider alternative treatments. Because Eastern medicine approaches the problem from a different logic, it has options, categories, and remedies for many conditions that seem to fall between the cracks of Western medicine.

Eastern medical theory looks at each problem as an individual case, even though the presenting symptoms seem similar. An example might clarify this. A typical sports injury is a pulled hamstring muscle, but to the Eastern healer, this diagnosis would be considered incomplete. Eastern healers look at many factors and try to discern patterns that make sense within the yin-yang theory. They study the problem as an interactive unity, to understand what led to this external symptom, the sore hamstring muscle.

One person who seeks treatment for a chronic hamstring pull might also be feeling fatigue with the pain. This individual has an uneven pulse, appears pale with clammy skin and a pasty tongue. This patient's hamstring pull could be viewed as overly yin, the result of blocked, stagnant chi that needs to be drained away, the blockage removed, and circulation of chi increased in the area. Energy flow would be enhanced with acupuncture needles or light acupressure on appropriate points along meridians that counteract this stagnant chi. Diet might be prescribed along with herbs such as ginseng. Chi kung could also be recommended to stimulate energy.

Another person with the same chronic hamstring symptom might be tense and flushed, with a "wiry" pulse quality and red tongue. The Eastern healer would look upon these signs as indicating an opposite meaning for the presenting symptom: overly active yang. Treatment for this individual would use different acupuncture or acupressure points and strategies. Needles and massage would be placed along meridian points to cool, calm, and relax, thereby helping the patient's chronically tight muscles to release their spasm. The doctor might suggest relaxing meditations and calming chi kung. The patient might also be given a prescription for a combination of herbs to calm and cool such as licorice or astragalus. In each case, the Eastern healer treats the unique pattern underlying the hamstring condition. Since the specific symptom is seen as a function of the whole person, a variety of interventions can help. The combinations are adjusted as the balance changes over time.

The accomplished healer attunes to the therapeutic process of the patient flexibly and sensitively, like a tai chi chuan master engaged in push hands (see Chapter 15). Symptoms mean something even though seemingly unrelated. Patients and any problems they might have are looked at and treated as a unit. Thus symptoms of a cold that might occur during the weeks of treatment for the pulled hamstring will also be addressed, relieving both simultaneously. Balance reasserts itself within the patient, gradually tipping the internal harmony of yin and yang back and forth until a dynamic flowing center is found.

AN ACUPUNCTURE TREATMENT SESSION

From the very first session patients receive treatment and usually experience relief. Eastern healers, however they intervene, will take a thorough history of the problem at the beginning of the first session. They then examine the patient, looking at the color of the tongue, feeling for several different pulses and varieties of pulse quality, and noting the patient's skin color. The healer also asks questions about energy and mood. Usually patients will feel surprised by the amount of detailed, sensitive attention to so many nuances and qualities that Western medicine ignores. These many observations help point the Eastern practitioner to the pervasive pattern affecting each individual patient. Such diagnosis is an art, learned by apprenticeship. Advanced practitioners add their intuition.

All the details of the exam are put together into a diagnosis, describing the difficulty in terms of elements, disharmonies, blockages, and other unusual categories. Sophisticated practitioners use complex maps. All of these relate to the theory of yin-yang balance, chi, flow through meridians, and the diagnosis interactions within the body and lifestyle of the particular patient.

The patient lies down on a padded table for the insertion of special needles. The needles are extremely fine, almost as thin as a human hair, and sterilized. The needles are placed all over the body even if the patient has a symptom in only one part of the body. Needles placed in the hand might paradoxically be felt in the foot if both are on the same meridian. The professional gently taps the needle in around a quarter of an inch and then twirls it carefully to stimulate chi circulation. Patients feel their chi sensation in various ways—tingling, warmth, or calm relaxation. After all the needles have been inserted, the acupuncturist leaves the patient to rest quietly for twenty minutes. This allows the treatment to take effect as the chi circulates. There may be a further twirling of needles during this time to affect the chi flow. The needles are then removed. Eastern doctors may prescribe certain herbs, diet, or exercise to help supplement treatment by acupuncture or acupressure. Most people leave their acupuncture session feeling relaxed and calm.

ACUPRESSURE THEORY

Acupressure and *tui na* massage of pressure points and meridians are an extension of acupuncture theory. Acupressure's effects may be somewhat milder than acupuncture, but good results have been obtained for many kinds of symptoms. No actual penetration of the points by needles is necessary.

In advanced massage methods, a sensitive and skilled practitioner can manipulate energy flow by tuning into the flow of energy in meridians with attentive "listening" hands and redirecting it. The healer may intensify the flow of chi into an area where it is deficient, or reduce or drain excess chi; or the patient may need to have an area unblocked by light pressure on appropriate points.

Some schools of acupressure such as Jin Shin recommend systematic applications of pressure to unblock key areas so that chi flow may be increased for healing or for the stimulation of a weakened function. The meridian that is next in the sequence of flow is also treated, a principle known as "Mother and Son," bringing about an increase of the desired effect. Other times the practitioner may choose to decrease chi flow to an area of hyperfunction—for example, to soothe an inflammation or calm an upset stomach.

Like acupuncture, the effects of acupressure may be enhanced by prescribing herbs that tend to soothe along with soothing treatments or stimulating herbs when this is more beneficial. Warming and cooling tendencies, as well as moistening and drying qualities are also present in herbs. These may be needed to encourage the patient's body to return to a dynamic balance.

Masters of acupressure can help to calm and tranquilize or to invigorate and energize a patient's weakened life force without significant pressure at all. Acupressure points can be easily learned and applied to everyday conditions. A skilled professional acupressurist may be able to guide you in your home treatment. Acupressure is not intended to substitute for traditional medical treatment, but it does work well along with it. Western medicine is used in modern China in conjunction with these methods, with excellent results.

Acupressure Techniques

You can do acupressure at home yourself to help relieve many pains and discomforts in conjunction with conventional medical treatment. Once correctly learned, you can apply the pressure to help cope with minor conditions such as relief of chronic pain, muscle spasms, tension headaches as an adjunctive nondrug treatment along with meditation, with no appreciable side effects.

Acupressure finger pressure should be light and comfortable, less than ten pounds. You should not feel any pain. Some schools use a small circling motion around the point in the meridian. Others prefer simple pressure, by pushing lightly with a finger or thumb.

APPLYING CHI KUNG TO HEALING

Chi kung can be used as an adjunct to healing. If you would like to use chi kung as part of your treatment regime, practice the chi kung exercises in Chapter 13. Then move on to the exercises included in this section. Some are specifically designed to move chi to the distressed area, helping to facilitate the healing process. One of the primary causes of illness, according to Eastern medicine, is stagnant or blocked chi. These exercises, combined with the techniques in Chapter 13, show how to get your chi moving again. These exercises are adjunctive and are not meant to substitute for conventional medical treatment.

Healthy Chi, Stagnant Chi Meditation

Sit quietly and breathe comfortably, without forcing your breaths. As you inhale, imagine that you are bringing in clean, fresh energy,

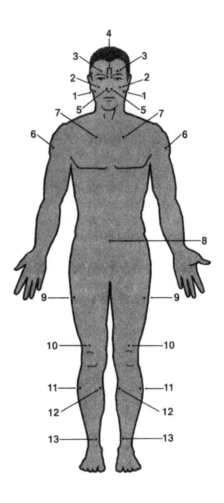

1. At lower edge of jaw, below ear (both sides).
   Massage circularly and then press lightly and steadily.
   For temporary relief from lower-tooth or jaw discomfort.

2. At cheekbone point (both sides).
   Massage and press.
   For temporary help with upper-tooth and jaw discomfort.

3. One inch above eyebrows (both sides).
   Massage and press.
   Dental and sinus discomfort.

4. Between eyebrows at bridge of nose (both sides).
   Squeeze between thumb and forefinger.
   Sinus congestion of colds or to stop a mild sneeze.

5. At nostrils both sides of nose.
   Press lightly.
   Nasal congestion.

6. Shoulder point.
   Massage and press.
   Shoulder, elbow, and arm pain.

7. Below collarbone between second and third ribs.
   Massage and press.
   Coughs.

8. Three inches below navel.
   Use circular motions, lightly massage the area, then light pressure.
   Abdominal discomfort.

9. Midlevel at outside of thigh (when standing, drop arms at your side, point is at the level of your middle finger).
   Massage then press.
   Tension in legs, hips, knees.

10. Two inches above kneecap.
    Massage and press.
    Abdominal and menstrual discomfort.

11. Outside of calf about four inches below knee.
    Massage and press.
    Lower leg, knee, ankle, and foot pains and strains.
    Encourages strengthening of these areas. Helps allergies.

12. Inside of calf. Massage and press.
    Lower leg, knee, ankle, and foot pains and strains.
    Encourages strengthening of these areas. Lower back discomfort.

13. Three inches above ankle.
    Stroke linearly.
    Menstrual discomfort and cramps.

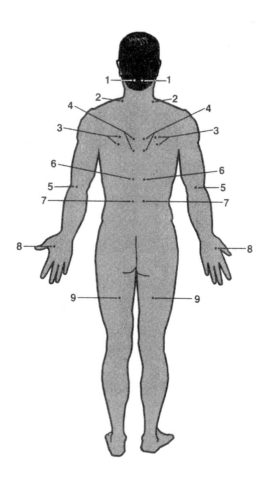

1. Below skull, top of both muscles of neck at the base of the skull.
Massage and press. Tension headaches, sinus congestion.

2. On trapezius, where shoulders and neck meet. Squeeze between thumb and fingers, then massage
Tight shoulders, overall tension, tension headaches.

3. Behind scapula. Stroke vertically between two sets of points. Upper back and shoulder strain.

4. Along two muscle strands. Stroke vertically between two sets of points. Upper middle back and shoulder strain.

5. Below elbow at hollow points between muscles.
Massage and press.
Wrist and arm discomfort, enhance immune system.

6. Below fourth and fifth ribs, on muscle bands. Massage then press. Helps with congestion, tight upper back, shoulders, and arms.

7. Lower back at second lumbar vertebrae, base of both muscles. Massage towards waist. For tight back if not injured.

8. Top of muscle on fork between thumb and index finger. Massage and press as in number 1. Helps with nasal congestion, colds, headaches, and dental discomfort.

9. Center of leg biceps. Massage then press. Tight muscles, menstrual discomfort.

positive chi. Hold your breath for several seconds and then exhale lightly; imagine that you are letting out the stagnant chi. With every breath you can feel yourself taking in the healthy, positive energy around you and expelling toxins and waste. Continue to breathe gently, in and out, allowing your vitality and feeling of well-being to be enhanced.

Directing Chi to Facilitate Healing

Sit and breathe comfortably for several minutes, performing the exercise above. Inhale the clean, fresh chi, hold briefly, and then exhale the old chi. Once you feel relaxed, inhale gently, directing the clean, fresh chi to the area that is bothering you. Hold the breath in this area for a specific number of counts, depending on where you are experiencing your difficulty. For problems in the digestion, including indigestion and diarrhea, as well as cold hands and feet, hold your breath for one count. For hypertension, hold for three counts. For urinary problems, hold for five counts. For colds and congestion, hold for seven counts. For headaches or fatigue, hold for nine counts. Finally, gently exhale, imaginatively moving the toxins away from the distressed area and out of your body. Continue for ten to fifteen minutes several times a day until the symptoms are relieved.

15

Martial Arts: Sources of Strategy

The martial arts without the Tao are like a face without eyes.
—Sang Kyu Shim

Chi, the power and force that is developed in martial arts to break boards and defend against aggressors, can also become the source of health and longevity. Not only have martial artists traditionally been healers, but Chinese healers usually practiced martial arts, and both used meditation. Early Taoists in China practiced martial arts, healing, and meditation altogether as one art.

The amazing feats of Taoist adepts due to the power of chi are legendary in Chinese history. Ancient stories tell of mysterious, seemingly frail old Taoist masters with great inner force who could send strong, young challengers flying through the air with a mere touch. One old master, Professor Wong, was able to poke holes in a sand-filled canvas kicking bag using only his index finger.

A great martial arts master lived in a small Chinese village, quietly practicing his art. All the villagers knew that he was truly wise and exceptionally strong even though he appeared old and frail. One day, a young challenger knocked loudly on the master's door. "People say you are very strong, but you look weak and old to me! I challenge you to a punching contest."

The master tried to talk the young man out of such a competition, but finally agreed to do it. The whole town gathered around to watch. The two men faced each other. "Please, you may go first," said the master quietly. The young man threw his most powerful punch directly into the stomach of the old master. The master took the punch with a serene look on his face. The younger man was surprised, but said, "OK, your turn!"

The master closed his eyes for a moment, gathering his chi, and then punched with what seemed to be a light touch. The young man yelled, then fell over, unconscious. The master knelt down to revive his opponent. When the young man woke up, he said with great respect in his voice, "Master, I have misjudged you. Please take me on as your student!" The former opponent became a loyal and dedicated student.

Such stories illustrate the martial applications of chi. Doctors were not always available after combat when needed. So the practitioners of martial arts learned healing techniques. Martial arts masters were often called upon to use their abilities with chi for healing, sometimes for their own students, sometimes for others. This gave another power to the martial arts teacher: not only to be able to cause discomfort, but also to be able to remove it. Change goes through a cycle of creation and destruction and back to creation, always in dynamic motion. The path of learning may be entered from many doorways. This tradition is still followed today. The training curriculum for a doctorate in Oriental medicine includes courses in Eastern internal martial arts such as tai chi chuan as well as the meditative internal energy art of chi kung.

TAI CHI CHUAN

Tai chi chuan is a martial art that expresses Taoism in movement. Though shrouded in mystery, the origins of tai chi chuan are said to have come from a fourteenth-century Taoist monk named Chang San-feng. The exact historical details are unclear, but he is credited as the founder because he was the first to bring Taoist principles to martial arts movements.

Chang San-feng was a large man, shaped like a turtle. He dressed only in priest robes and let his beard grow long. He could eat an entire bushel of food or be without any food for weeks at a time. He lived simply in a small cottage and traveled around the Wu Dan Mountain with his disciple.

One legend tells how Chang San-feng was summoned by Emperor Wei Tsung to come to his castle and teach him his martial art. Chang San-feng set out on the journey but found the road blocked, making passage impossible. That night the emperor dreamt that he was taught the martial art. At dawn the emperor reputedly defeated one hundred enemies single-handed! This story shows the Taoist character of Chang San-feng's teachings, tai chi chuan was learned in a dream.

Tai chi chuan became more widely disseminated in the 1800s and evolved into three branches called Ch'en, Yang, and Wu. Ch'en is the oldest form and derives directly from the teachings of Chang San-feng. Yang Lu Ch'an (1799–1872) went to Honan Province to learn the old Ch'en style. He founded a school in Peking where he taught his own branch of tai chi chuan called the Yang style. He passed his art along to his sons who continued to teach the Yang style and helped spread tai chi chuan widely.

One of Yang Lu Ch'an's sons taught a man named Wu Yu-hsiung. Wu also journeyed to study with a Ch'en master and was given a copy of an ancient tai chi manual, reputedly passed along for generations. He combined the styles of Yang and Ch'en to create the third style, which is now called Wu. He also wrote several books that combined the principles of the older manual with his own interpretations. Sayings from these books are often quoted or paraphrased to express the internal theoretical bases and external criteria of tai chi chuan.

Wu's manual, *The Elucidation of the Thirteen Kinetic Move-*

ments, described how tai chi movements should be performed and how the mind of the practitioner should be applied. These qualities can be deduced from Taoist principles. If practitioners follow Tao, their tai chi chuan reaches a high level. The tai chi chuan sequence is a natural extension of Taoist principles.

The three branches of tai chi chuan all derive from each other, based on the original root style. Thus, in keeping with Taoist philosophy, from Tao came the One, from the One came Two, from the Two came Three, and from the Three, "The 10,000" styles and practitioners of today have evolved.

PRINCIPLES OF TAI CHI CHUAN

In every movement the entire body should be light and agile and all of its parts connected like a string of pearls.
–Tai Chi Classics

Tai chi chuan draws its general principles from Taoist concepts. The flowing wordless wisdom of Tao is communicated with flowing motions of hands and feet. Practitioners strive to move with grace and balance, and guide the patterning movements by the principles of Tao.

Internal power generated by chi kung is the basis for tai chi chuan technique. Exert no unnecessary strength; be continuous. "To hold back is to release; continuity should not cease" (Wu, in Lee 1968, 52). Not only are the movements performed in continuous sequence, but the practitioner's entire body is coordinated to move in unison: "Every joint of the entire body must be linked together so that there is not the least interruption" (Lee 1968, 59).

In tai chi chuan technique, yin and yang are always kept in flowing harmony. Left is followed by right, upward by downward, in hand and foot patterns. Yielding, noncontending, Oneness with the opponent and oneself, help practioners remain in balance. To accomplish this, practioners learn to maintain what is called the solid and empty factors. "The solid and empty factors must be distinctly differentiated. In each and every phase there must be these two factors." In a legendary story, one of Yang's sons demonstrated how the solid and empty factors worked. He placed a bird on his open palm. Every time the bird tried to spread its wings and push off against his hand for flight, Yang yielded just the right amount, so that the bird could not fly away. The bird seemed to be stuck to Yang's palm. Tai chi chuan power is deceptive: Muscles are relaxed, motion is formless and curved, yet the practitioner is unstoppable when performing techniques correctly.

Tai chi chuan practitioners practice the motions in a set series of patterns called a form. Personal instruction through imitation of the master's movements help students learn these patterns. The number varies from the original 108 movements to shorter and longer modified versions. Each movement is performed meditatively, with mind and body working together. You can experiment with this principle by meditating on movement in the exercises that follow.

TAI CHI CHUAN EXERCISES

Included here are some simple patterns drawn from the classic tai chi chuan form. Practice these until you can do them from memory. Let your body remain loose and rounded, as you did in the chi kung exercises. If you find that you like these movements, you may want to consider taking a tai chi chuan class.

Posture 1: Raise Hands

Stand with your feet shoulder width apart and arms at your sides. Relax your mind and body. Raise both arms slowly with palms facing the floor until you reach shoulder height, inhaling gently. Then gently press both hands downwards until they come all the way back down, with palms still facing the floor. Keep your head lifted slightly upwards as you exhale lightly. Movements should be light, slow, and continuous.

Posture 2: Parting the Horse's Mane
Draw your arms gently back toward your waist. In one continuous motion, turn to the right as you step to your right foot, bending the right knee. At the same time push forward with your right hand, palm facing you while you sweep the left hand downward out from your side. Let your weight shift slightly forward as you push. Maintain the natural curve of your elbows in both arms.

Bring your hands back as you bring your foot back to shoulder width, parallel position. Then step forward with the left foot and repeat the pattern. All motions should be slow and continuous, one melting into the next.

Repeat patterns several times.

TAI CHI MEDITATION
When performed in the traditional Taoist way, tai chi chuan is a form of moving meditation. The source for movement is not exertion of muscle strength; chi directed by your mind is far more powerful. You move with tranquillity as your chi circulates through your body. This exercise shows you how to link mind and body, allowing natural movement to happen.

Stand with feet shoulder width apart and close your eyes. Imagine one of the patterns from the tai chi chuan exercises. Picture yourself doing it, but do not move on purpose. Relax your body and allow yourself to move in the pattern you are imagining. Do not force it. Can you let your body move effortlessly, almost as if it is moving by itself?

PUSH HANDS

Students eventually progress in training to a stage of interaction with a partner, called Push Hands, or T'ui Shou. When the arm of the partner moves, the tai chi chuan practitioner follows, learning to listen with the sense of touch. Eventually, training brings such sensitivity that a skilled practitioner can anticipate the partner's motion before they take place. This ability parallels Taoism empathetic sensitivity to external conditions.

Push Hands Exercise

You can enhance your sensitivity to another using this exersise. This can be useful for sensing force directed toward you. When you are truly aware of the other person, the Taoist way of non-contending becomes clear. Think of this exercise as a metaphor for a conflict situation. Can you stay attuned without contending?

Face your partner. Let your partner be the guide and you be the one to follow. The guide raises an arm, extending the hand forward. Place your hand lightly over your partner's wrist and close your eyes. Your partner moves his or her arm around slowly, back and forth, up and down. You stay with your partner's hand; lightly moving in unison. Can you sense the force of movement without adding any force of your own.

After several minutes, switch roles. This exercise can be done with each hand as well. Both people should remain relaxed at all times.

This exercise illustrates noncontending. Awareness, in touch with the force, does not interfere with the course of things as they are. In so doing, a change takes place and the situation is resolved naturally.

JUDO, AIKIDO, AND TAE CHUN DO INCORPORATE TAOIST PRINCIPLES

In the *internal* arts, meditative focus is primary. External form is always secondary to the internal focus. Some of the other martial arts, such as judo, aikido, and tae chun do follow the Taoist principles as well.

JUDO

Jigaro Kano systemized and codified his own form of the older grappling art jujitsu by organizing a few basic principles into a style known as Kodokan Judo. Judo was subsequently widely taught throughout Japan and eventually worldwide, achieving Olympic event status. Lao-tzu's conception of yielding can be understood as actual physical forces interacting.

The primary principle of judo is that a strong offensive force should not be resisted. Instead, practitioners learn to yield and flow with it, so that the aggressor's own force can be used against him. This principle was formulated succinctly by Kano as the Principle of Maximum Efficiency. Kano believed his principle was applicable universally.

If the opponent pushes and you push back, the stronger force wins, often at great cost. If instead, you pull as he pushes, you gain the advantage of the other's force and can overcome with only a small force of your own. Throwing your opponent becomes possible. Aggressive motion towards another requires energy and leads to an imbalance. Thus, paradoxically you gain by losing ground. You then use your force much more efficiently, and a smaller force may overcome a larger one. This principle can be applied in many of life's situations, such as business, fixing things, and even interpersonally.

AIKIDO

Aikido also drew from Taoist concepts and early jujitsu techniques, combining and refining a distinctive style through the broad knowledge and sensitive spirituality of the founder, Moreyu Uyeshiba. Uyeshiba organized his art around a spiritually symbolic principle that transcended the battle situation: keeping in the center, extending positive flowing energy, in harmony and calmness. When harmony is broken, the aikidoist steps in to restore it. Opponents are sent spinning, often in flight, and taken down into locks that render them helpless. Well into his eighties, Uyeshiba was still able to demonstrate masterful control over four attackers rushing him simultaneously.

The highest level of the aikido art is to bring about defeat without harm to the practitioner or the attacker. The intent of practioners is to be meditatively serene and maintain peace and harmony with the universe. Aggressive attacks by an opponent break harmony. The practitioner seeks to restore the harmony. The ideal response is graceful yet devastating to the aggressor.

The aikidoist meets and follows the opponent's attacking energy, referred to as *ki* (the Japanese translation of the Chinese "chi"), and joins with it. The practitioner finds a safe direction to lead the attack, and then flows into a series of dynamic movements that ultimately draw the attacker away from successful attack and into submission, gracefully leading the attack into neutrality. Flowing circular or spiraling motions are characteristic. Aikidoists sensitize themselves to the direction of energy and extend positively, whether toward an opponent or in everyday life. Techniques sometimes overlap with judo and jujitsu, but aikido's flow and philosophical applications have a unique, unmistakable character.

Tae Chun Do

Tae chun do, a contemporary martial art, harmonizes yin and yang, active and passive, offense and defense. Choice of application varies with the situation, the person, and the reaction. Practitioners create sensitive strategies to solve the problem of the situation as perceived. Each situation is unique, calling sometimes for yielding with a soft yin-type response, sometimes for opposition from a dynamic, forceful yang response. The practitioner remains balanced, neutralizing the opponent's force in whatever way is necessary and natural. This approach accords with the Taoist way of being One with the nature of things, whatever they may be, and then responding harmoniously.

TAOIST STRATEGY

A further development from martial arts is application of the principles of Tao to strategy. These strategies can be applied practically to everyday life situations.

Taoist values permitted strategic maneuvering and deception in martial arts, as shown in *The Art of War* by Sun-tzu, a manual of military advice and strategy that is believed by contemporary scholars to have been written circa fourth century B.C.E., but whose actual authorship in literal terms, as usual in Taoist texts, is in question. Taoists prefer the mysterious as the truer source of wisdom. The perspective given by the book, though, is clearly that of a Taoist skilled in the ways of war.

The Art of War has been a guide to tactics and concepts for study for more than two thousand years, in classical China and feudal Japan, as well as modern times. Throughout history the text was required study by Asian and, later, Western scholars in order to comprehend war strategy, as well as formulate it. Chairman Mao analyzed and drew from concepts articulated in this book for his successful strategy and tactics. But strategic concepts transcend the context of war.

According to Sun-tzu's theory, the general must weigh the situation before moving so that he can adapt to changing conditions. The Taoist approach to action, flexible yet implacable, is like a flowing river of force, sweeping away all resistance in its path, or else flowing around it.

Taoist strategy approaches problem-solving situations with methods drawn from opposites. At higher levels of sophistication, martial arts combat is ultimately a battle of minds. Interpersonal conflicts can also be viewed in this way. Ultimately, a meeting of minds brings about the best resolution.

Moving as intangibly as a ghost in the light, he is obscure, inaudible. His primary target is the mind of the opposing commander; the victorious situation, a product of his creative imagination. Sun-Tzu realized than an indispensable preliminary to battle was to attack the mind of the enemy.

Strategy can be both direct and indirect. Cheng and *ch'i* are the dual concepts that Sun-tzu used to classify strategic action, corresponding to direct and indirect action. Cheng is direct attack; ch'i, indirect. Cheng may be orthodox, confrontational. Ch'i is surprising, unorthodox, devious. When near the skilled general seems far; when far, near. When the skilled general attacks, it is swift and unexpected, yet devious, moving away in such a manner as to unbalance the opponent, then moving in close before the opponent is prepared. The victorious solution is reached by balancing the opposites. But each balance is individual. Situations and their needs vary. Sensitivity, accurate assessment, and good judgement are necessary.

Since Tao is without form in its own true nature, outer events and circumstances, as the sage responds to them, give form to the flexible Tao. Be like water, without shape, Sun-tzu counseled:

And as water shapes its flow in accordance with the ground, so an army manages its victory in accordance with the situation of the enemy. And as water has no constant form, there are in war no constant conditions.

React to the situation without any fixed purpose of your own. Respond to the requirements of external conditions and circumstances as they are. Modify strategy and tactics according to what is needed. This advice has applications in all aspects of life, both at home with family and out in the world of interaction.

Ultimately, the Taoist sage, in all of life's confrontations, seeks the path of noncontention, the peaceful way. Sun-tzu recognized this and set it as the highest expression of his art:

For to win 100 victories in 100 battles is not the acme of skill. To subdue the enemy without fighting is the acme of skill.

16
Creative Arts: Expressing Tao

*The fusion of yin and yang at the Center comes in a moment
of self-mastery, in love or in artistic creation; one may find it
in calligraphy, in poetry, dance or all other forms of art.*
— Kristofer Schipper

TAOIST ARTS

The formless, nameless Tao is the source of creation. Artists draw
upon the Tao for creativity. When artists identify with Tao, they
perceive beyond superficial appearances into deeper essence. Taoism has inspired many artists through the ages. Taoist painting,
with its own character and style, has been practiced over centuries.
Some forms of modern architecture also draw upon Taoist principles. Let these artistic expressions inspire you.

Taoist Painting

Painting has expressed Tao in China for thousands of years. Since
Tao is nonconceptual, one way to express it and give others an
experience of it is through art. Chi is always in motion and must
flow freely. Techniques were developed to express this through the
feeling artists had of their subject. Flowing, beautiful brush strokes
express and extend chi in the artist's visions.

Art theorists wrote of composition in terms of yin and yang
harmony to inspire a more balanced picture. Yin and yang qual-

ities were ascribed to objects. For example, the solid yang mass of rocks could be rendered by using solid thick strokes. Clouds, vapor, and mist, which partake of yin character, could be rendered by using diffuse wash strokes. But the center, the origin of these, is the vital breath, the artist's spirit, expressed in brush strokes. Flowing the breath of chi as well as representing symbols of yin and yang in objects and techniques of painting came to be a pivotal part of Chinese painting.

Several great painters—K'u K'ai Shih (344–406), Tsung Ping (373–443), and Wang Wei (415–443)—wrote essays, inspired by Taoist spirituality, describing their approach to painting. But these ideas were not systematic, formalized, or categorized until Hsieh Ho formulated the definitive descriptive categories of painting, known as the Six Canons, in his work *Ku Hua P'in Lu* (Record of the Classification of Painters, 500 C.E.). Ho's categories became the standard that all artists had to come to terms with in their work. Later painters and art theorists interpreted and enlarged on the Six Canons, but they remained the bedrock of theory.

Each of the Six Canons communicates a pair of principles to guide artists in their approach to painting. Written in classical form, each canon consists of six characters. The first four give the instruction or statement. The last confirms the teaching by stating *shih yeh*, meaning, "so be it." Throughout history these conceptions were interpreted various ways, but always remain anchored to the Six Canons.

The first two canons establish the origin and basis for painting technique within the Tao. Canon One expresses the central philosophical position of all: chi yun, shen tung, shih yeh—chi revolving, life stirs, so be it. One interpretation, of the many that have been given through the ages, is that the circulation of chi produces life movement. Once the painter is in tune with Tao, the brush moves, inspired with spirit. Specific techniques are explained in the third, fourth, fifth, and sixth canons. Later, chi yun (chi revolving) became an important concept in Chinese painting and a criterion to evaluate works of art. The spirit shen should be revealed, stirred to motion. Shen tung expresses this principle. The inner breathes life into form through action.

> *The true artist, as well as the true poet, is not concerned with the likeness of form, but aims at bringing forth the rhythm that pulsates within it, and then is carried forth to the beholder.*
> —Chung-yuan Chang

K'u K'ai Shih wrote in a historic essay that the purpose of painting is to reveal the character of the spirit. He believed the best understanding is to permit an interactive experience with the painting. While gazing at the work of art, a viewer should allow the spirit of the painting to communicate itself.

Letting Go to the Flow of Chi: Automatic Drawing and Writing

Taoist art flows from the center—letting your chi move you. This exercise will help you do this. Many people have experienced automatic drawing or writing while doing something else. For example, have you ever found yourself doodling without really thinking about it while talking on the telephone? This ability to let yourself move automatically can be used to help you foster creativity the Taoist way.

If you are a painter, ready your paints. For poets and writers, get out paper and pen.

First perform some of the chi exercises from Chapter 13. When you feel some tingling in your hands, sit down in front of your work. Place the brush or pen in your hand. Close your eyes and imagine your chi flow increasing. Let the tingling or warmth move up your arms if you can. Place the pen or brush on the paper. Imagine that the pen begins to move of itself. You do not move deliberately. Simply wait and allow your hand to move of itself. If you are a painter, wait for your brush to stroke the paper. Writers and poets, allow your hand to write words. Let your mind relax, think of nothing in particular. Do not interfere with your natural abilities.

FENG SHUI

A factory was having difficulty with productivity. Workers were disgruntled. Work was going slowly. The manager had tried every logical solution he could think of, with no success. In desperation, he called in a renowned consultant. The expert came in, looked around carefully, but said nothing. The manager watched impatiently as the consultant stood and walked around the factory. Finally, after an entire day spent in silence, looking, walking, and listening to the workers, the consultant asked for $1,000, his fee for services. After he received it, he advised, "Open the window in the assembly room of the factory and all will be well." The manager felt cheated. The price seemed high, an expensive charge for a foolish solution to his serious problem, but he reluctantly complied. Within a few days the atmosphere at the factory mysteriously began to change. Workers felt happier. The open window circulated fresh air into the factory. They had always wanted this. They felt listened to and more comfortable, within and without. They worked harder. In only a few months, production doubled! The manager acknowledged that indeed the price was low.

According to Feng Shui theory, this simple solution unblocked the flow of chi that was needed, returning the factory building to harmony with the vital forces and the workers to harmony with their administrators. Then the flow of work production could increase as well.

Feng Shui works with both the interior and exterior design of a building and the surrounding area to bring them in harmony with natural forces. Experts in Feng Shui train to become sensitive to the internal energy of chi, so that they can notice the subtle impact it has on the interaction between the house and its environment, including the different rooms, furniture, building, and even the people who live there. Over time, relatively stable concepts and principles of organizing and arranging objects and life spaces were discovered and incorporated into Feng Shui.

Development of Feng Shui

Feng Shui translates as "wind" and "water," natural forces in our world and can be traced back to occult practices that were part of the early Taoist sects. Although Chinese occultism was based on superstition, there was a scientific component to it as well. Occult practitioners were searching for ways to harness the forces of nature, just as science does today. However, the definition of what constituted forces of nature included both the natural and supernatural. Modern science overlaps with occult sciences when little understood supernatural forces become understood with time and research to become redefined as natural phenomena.

The first book about Feng Shui was written in 600 C.E. Called *The Water-Dragon Classic*, it described the Water-Dragon School of Feng Shui, which studied water surrounding a plot of land. Another Feng Shui manual was composed around 850 by an imperial Feng Shui master and Chinese scholar named Yang Yun Sung who founded the Shapes and Form School of Feng Shui. He based his instructions on the features of land. Two centuries later, another school of Feng Shui, the Compass School, analyzed flat planes and their effects on placement of buildings. A later school that developed during the Northern Sung period (960–1126) was called the Fukien School. This style added analysis based on time and orientation of directions. Feng Shui began as an occult art centered in the supernatural, but it evolved into a Taoist art with practical usefulness today.

Underlying Principle of Feng Shui

Modern Feng Shui practitioners accept the Tao as their founding principle: We are One with the universe—One with Tao. Since we are One with our environment, we resonate with it. Our environment can have significant effects on how we feel and function. When disharmony occurs, negative things happen. Life must flow freely and chi must circulate. Blockages of chi are not healthy. Where windows are placed, the direction the front door faces, the shape of the rooms, how furniture is arranged, and many other factors can alter how well chi flows, and how we flow with Tao in our everyday lives, within us and as a part of the world around us.

Feng Shui Exercise

Here is a simple exercise that you can do in your own home to apply Feng Shui principles. Sometimes the way we open windows in the house can interfere with the circulation of chi through the rooms. If one window is lined up directly across from another, chi will be blown straight through the house with no opportunity to circle around within. Feng Shui experts recommend putting a barrier between the two windows, so that the chi is forced to circulate before leaving.

ORGANIC ARCHITECTURE

The reality of a room was to be found in the space enclosed by the roof and walls, not in the roofs and walls themselves.
                                                            –Kakuzo Okakura

Frank Lloyd Wright, founder of organic architecture, revolutionized architecture with the principles in his work. He naively thought he invented organic architecture's founding principle. Later, when someone gave him Okakura's classic work *The Book of Tea*, he recognized that the basic principle he thought he invented had been known long before him by Lao-tzu. At first his pride was deflated, but he renewed his confidence when he realized that he had brought these brilliant ideas to life:

I had thought of myself as an original, but was not. It took me days to swell up again. But I began to swell up again when I thought, After all, who built it? Who put that thought into buildings? Laotse nor anyone else had consciously built it.

Organic architecture embodies timeless values that are fundamental to Taoism, such as naturalness, simplicity, and wholeness, recasting them in modern form. Inner space, the emptiness within, permits the life force of the house—its chi, to take form. The space within the whole is central, not external details of construction such as walls, ceiling, or ornaments. Lao-tzu would have approved.

The interrelationship of house to site is an integral part of organic designs. The organic house, as Wright envisioned it, should be simple, made of natural materials, related to its surroundings and the person who would be living in it. All were taken into account in Wright's organic design. He minimized decorations and ornamentation, except when they expressed the theme of the house or room. Walls, floor, and roof came together as a whole rather than in additive fashion. Wherever possible, beams and posts in walls or ceiling were eliminated. For example, in the Imperial Hotel in Tokyo, the floor of each story, made with massive concrete cast sections, was the ceiling of the next. Wright's designs emphasized the unity of the structure through its function. He believed that the essence of a house is found in its unity as a whole rather than from the details of its features. Like Taoism, which finds the usefulness of a cup in its emptiness, the space within the house was a guiding functional value to Wright.

> *The idea of organic architecture, that the reality of the building lies in the space within to be lived in, the feeling that we must not enclose ourselves in an envelope which is the building, is not alone Oriental. Democracy, proclaiming the integrity of the individual per se, had the feeling if not the words.*

Wright wanted to help make the American dream of everyone owning their own home a reality. He proposed to build good designs that were affordable and available to people of moderate income through organic principles. His early designs permitted houses to be built, in the early 1900s, for as little as $5,000! He continued to create until 1959. Chuang-tzu wrote that if people could live in a simple way, all would be happy and fulfilled. He envisioned a society where everyone had adequate shelter without excess. Wright attempted to put that theory into practice.

Wright pointed out that organic designs must be very individualistic. Each home was uniquely suited to the individual client, the environmental area and application, and their personal dignified use of the design as their home. Wright conceptualized buildings as connected to their conditions, rooted in the building's origins, a response to the situation. As Lao-tzu said, "To know harmony is to be in accord with the eternal." Wright's success with this approach demonstrates that Taoist principles are useful and practical.

Wright understood organic architecture as the embodiment of function in form. Form and function are not in sequence to Wright. They are One. This unity of form in function becomes wholeness.

If form really "followed function" as the Master declared—here was the direct means of expression that form and function are one: the only true means I could see then or can see now to eliminate the separation and complication of cut-and-butt joinery in favor of the expressive flow of continuous surface.

Continuity is part of the basic essence of Tao. Wright wanted flowing of unity in his designs, without punctuating them by structural details that broke up the Oneness. He even wanted furniture built into his houses to reduce clutter and unify all the parts.

The principle of organic unity in architecture as in art itself was recognized and written about by the renowned American sculptor Horatio Greenough before 1850 (Greenough, in Small 1947). Greenough coined the phrase "Form follows function." Beauty is not found in ultimate ideal forms to copy and adapt that conform to some external standard. According to Greenough, the form as a whole should express its function. The promise of function, when fulfilled by expression as action, is the source of beauty in an object.

We judge a form as beautiful when it fulfills its function. For example, we experience a graceful Arabian horse with a powerful gait as beautiful, just as a finely tuned sports car may also be beautiful. Each form is unique, beautiful in its own way. We would probably experience an old arthritic horse as less beautiful unless it is a family pet. Similarly, a beat-up, broken-down clunker of a car is less than beautiful to us. Beauty is experienced from synchrony with function. The actual presence of this potential for perfection in motion creates a visible harmony that is pleasing. We experience the expression of the true inner nature as beautiful. Beauty emerges when the form is true to its inner nature, permitting the unimpeded flow of its potential perfection into actual expression. Vitality should be expressed in action.

Good design has value beyond its use within the object itself. The harmony of design styles with their true inner spirit calls out in us a similar harmony with our own true nature. If decorations are added that do not belong to the unified spirit of the design, they detract from its integrity, and we feel it. We may notice it intuitively as a lack of beauty, or as something "off," or it may seem "wrong" somehow, though we may not quite know why. We resonate with harmonious design. We feel calm and at one within a well-designed form. Integration of the details within the whole becomes a useful criterion for architecture, as in any work of art.

Greenough believed that careful observation followed by study of the deeper principles behind architecture itself would reveal general principles of design. He stated that these general principles found within should be the basis of individual designs. He did not mean to encourage people to eliminate detail that is necessary. Simplicity requires good judgment. Frank Lloyd Wright, in his theoretical statements, embraced and extended these concepts as well. Delete extraneous detail, he counseled. Permit the design to speak for itself.

> *To know what to leave out and what to put in; just where and just how, ah, that is to have been educated in knowledge of simplicity—toward ultimate freedom of expression.*

Simplicity was important to Frank Lloyd Wright in the twentieth century, to Greenough in the nineteenth century, to the Taoists before 600 B.C.E., and to us. The value of simplicity leads us back to the spirit of Tao, timeless, and as relevant today as it was then. Tao enhances art as well as design as it stirs us with its vitality.

17

Being Whole: Returning to the Way to Find Balance

Intuition is no more a supernatural gift than the powers of walking, running, and jumping, but like them, its full development requires regular exercise.
—I Ching

RETURNING TO INNER HARMONY BY NOT KNOWING

When seeking to make a change, people are often eager to do something about it right away. Common sense counsels: Do it now! But the effort to try to change sets up a struggle, leading to imbalance. Taoism suggests a different mind-set. Let it be. Begin with acceptance. Then a paradox emerges.

When you stop resisting and go with the flow, the natural order reasserts itself; change begins. Life's process is flowing through continuous cycles from creation to a peak of being, to destruction, from birth, to maturity, to death. Trust in this process. Continue to play your part faithfully and change begins to take place of itself.

Stop trying to force the inner essence to emerge, to impose form. Inner essence is in process and should be allowed to take its natural form. If you want to grow beautiful flowers in a garden, plant the seeds, give them the conditions they need: adequate soil, water, sun, fertilizer, and proper temperature. As the plant grows, tend to it and let it grow. If you pull on the plants to make them grow taller, they wither and die. Overwater them or overfertilize them and the plants will not grow better. Living things need the conditions they need: no more, no less. You do not need to add your force. Be still (wu-wei); let go of useless activity (yu-wei).

Return to Tao and a gap is created, an openness through the unknown. But first, for the unknown to be, the known, that which is, must not be. Return to the mode of not-knowing, not-doing. This permits the inner essence to emerge. Mysteriously, matters begin to resolve.

Milton Erickson, one of the world's most innovative hypnotherapists, used his capacities in unique and unusual ways. When he was stuck or blocked with a patient, he enjoyed calling on his personal creativity to help. Sometimes he would go into trance before the next session with that problematic patient, and bring about in himself, by suggestion, a state of not-knowing. He could cause himself to forget who the patient was. Erickson believed that creative forgetting permits people to experience new potentials. When the patient arrived for therapy, Erickson greeted the patient as a new patient, and began as if for the first time. New ideas and options for the patient were free to occur to him.

The first time we meet someone, we often have an intuitively clear sense of them. As time passes, our habitual experiences with this person can interfere with insightful, original first impressions. Through the wisdom of not knowing, Taoism helps us become more perceptive.

You can discover new options, open new possibilities with each situation. Previous knowledge and resulting concepts may lead to narrow possibilities from rigid constraints. On the other hand, we are often more aware, spontaneous, and perceptive when we do something or meet someone for the first time. We have no sense yet of the boundaries, and therefore we can be open-minded and creative. Children are often creative and bold: The young child is experiential and does not know yet of fixed constraints.

You can train to use your unconscious functioning and become greatly skilled. Rely on your instinctual abilities with confidence. Each of us has talents, training, and abilities we can apply instinctually to our own problematic life situations. We need to be open to unlearn what we know, to understand in a new way. The Taoist approach requires less of learning, in the sense of accumulating knowledge. Learning may be an impediment.

Exercise: Return to Not-Knowing

Sit quietly with your eyes closed. Think back on the first time you met someone who is important to you. Recall what you thought, how you experienced the person, and what he or she meant to you then. Compare this to how you know this individual now, with all the interactions you have shared. Is your first intuitive impression different or has it remained true for how you experience the person now?

Exercise in Not-Knowing

This exercise is best done when you have an hour or two of free time. Go to a museum of your choosing—for example, an art museum. When you get there, let yourself wander around without anything in mind. Look at what is there and let your natural reactions guide you as to what to do next. Wander from room to room. Look at the art that you feel drawn to see. Do not force yourself to analyze the art. You can vary this by going to a park or a library without having any purpose in mind. Experiment with not-knowing and simply experience.

KNOWLEDGE VS. WISDOM

The usual approach to knowing something is to define it, specify the objectives, determine the goals to be accomplished. When working on a problem, we first like to classify or diagnose it in order to determine the course of action to take.

How can we make sure that our categories are the correct ones? Often, in our modern age, with all the learning that is possible, increasing all the time, people can confuse knowledge and wisdom. Knowledge is not wisdom and wisdom is not knowledge. Greatly knowledgable people exist, the product of learning from books or school. They may have memorized many facts about a particular subject, but, over time, have become estranged from their intuitive, inner grasp of the unity which comes with wisdom. Then again, some are wise even though they have had little education and memorized few facts. Wisdom does not necessarily come with learning facts or memorizing data. Lao-tzu points to this in silence.

Wisdom has great value, adding a capacity for flexible resilience in life and with other people. Wisdom helps show when we should take action and when it is better to do nothing except let nature take its course. Good parents know that they must stand back and not interfere, to allow their children to grow and mature for themselves. This lesson can be difficult to accept—for example, when your child is dressing herself too slowly and you are late. Taking charge and dressing her yourself might feel more comfortable at that moment, but letting go of parental control to allow your daughter to learn for herself will have lasting benefits.

The Way to Tao, then, is not through knowing and doing but rather through not-knowing and nondoing. This opens the door to Tao.

YIELDING AND NONCONTENDING

Anger and resentment are sometimes a function of expecting ourselves or others to be perfect: "They should not do this," we tell ourselves, silently. "They should know better." But at times we must accept their imperfections as well as our own, so that we can endure and withstand, and then go on.

Exercise in Inner Noncontending

Give yourself some time to be silent, to quietly reflect on a problematic circumstance. For these moments there is no answer yet, no solution to the problem. Wait; have faith in not-knowing. The unknown is a gap, a hole in the fabric of continuity. In that gap, new potentials can emerge. Leave open space for this to take place. Do not argue with yourself about the fact that you face an unknown. The Taoist principle of noncontending applies to your inner thoughts just as much as it does in the outer circumstance. When you let go of knowing, you give the answers an opportunity to flow.

Yielding and noncontending can become an important skill when applied interpersonally. Respect for nature in ourselves encourages respect for nature in others, too. Sometimes nature requires space to manifest latent potential. If we learn to let the other be, we can bring about peace through a gentler, more tender attitude. By yielding respectfully to both our own and the other's needs, we can resolve differences.

Realizing our own similarity with others implies a willingness to let ourselves and others be incomplete at times, not perfect, as part of the balance. This willingness to let be may need to be extended from ourselves to others, a difficult attitude to cultivate in these ambitious times of expected high achievement. Taoist wisdom counsels us not to rush too quickly into decisions. Answers take time to come. We also should not push others into rigid attitudes, or too quickly give answers. Patience, the Taoists tell us. Wait. Heaven and Earth will correct of themselves.

WU-WEI OF THE PSYCHE

Modern life puts an emphasis on conscious intellectual development, often submerging the irrational unconscious mind. When we go too far in this direction, we create an imbalance: too much yang without enough yin. When too overbalanced in the conscious intellect, problems spring up, seemingly out of nowhere. Carl Jung recognized this when he said: "Be that as it may, the fact remains that a consciousness heightened by an inevitable one-sidedness gets so far out of touch with the primordial images that a breakdown occurs."

Psychologists' offices are filled with people who have rejected one part of their personality in the interest of another. Midlife depression is common. Sometimes those who seem to be the most successful and disciplined find themselves plagued with anxieties, boredom, or dissatisfaction with life.

People should accept themselves fully, including their unconscious dreaming mind. We express ourselves both in conscious aware thoughts and feelings, and in unconscious dreams that are beyond the threshold of awareness. The interplay of yin and yang must be free to express itself naturally.

Mental health comes when we allow our psyche to be, trusting the process to unfold. Then disharmony within dissolves. We stop having inner battles, where one part of the personality struggles against another. Our inner being finds its natural balance, like water finding its level, and we function in harmony with ourselves and the world.

By accepting and staying with the natural flow of experience, with nothing in mind and not doing anything to alter it, things change. For example: A client consulted us because she suffered from disturbing nightmares. She dreamed that horrible monsters were chasing her, and she was terrified. The dream recurred often. She was a very sweet person who spoke softly. In the course of therapy she disclosed that she never expressed any anger because she rejected it, utterly. She believed being angry was an ugly, negative emotion.

She feared that if she ever allowed herself to get angry she would become overly aggressive. She had willed her emotions into check, or so she thought. As Taoism would predict, the aggressive, yang feelings would not go away.

Instead, they came back to frighten her in her dreams. We encouraged her to stop tinkering with her own personality and to return to her natural being, before yin and yang. She learned how to stop controlling herself and let her feelings flow naturally. At first, she felt her emotions very intensely, which made her a little uncomfortable. Soon she lost her discomfort. She was far from being the overly aggressive person she had feared. Instead, as the rest of her personality came into balance with the rejected hidden part of her, she found a way to express the full range of her emotions without losing her sweet, calm disposition. Her nightmares disappeared: Her monster had been her own anger fighting to be heard. What seemed so overwhelming to her, once accepted and embraced within her total personality, found harmony. The exercises that follow will guide you gently back to a center.

Flowing with Awareness Exercise

In this exercise you let things happen and simply follow the flow of awareness. Notice what you experience, think, and feel, but do not do anything to change it. Follow the path of your awareness, no matter how the path may seem to zigzag. Your intellect may jump in to belittle a thought, "Oh what a stupid idea," or may even try to change your thinking, "I shouldn't be thinking that." Set aside your judgments.

Be sensitive to any fantasies or imaginings, even if they are mere flickers into consciousness. If you lose awareness of the flow, gently bring yourself back to it and resume. Begin with five to ten minutes and increase the time up to thirty minutes.

PATHWAY TO THE TAO : THE UNCONSCIOUS

> *The dream is a spontaneous self-portrayal in symbolic form, of the actual situation in the unconscious.*
>
> –Carl Jung

"Dreams are the royal road to the unconscious," Sigmund Freud wrote. Dreams have been used by many great psychologists—Freud, Jung, and Fritz Perls, founder of Gestalt therapy—to interpret and guide the inner life. Thousands of years ago, Taoist sages were using dreams to help people find their path back to unconscious wisdom.

Guided Daydream Warm-Up

Learning to work with your unconscious mind is a skill that responds to practice. Accept the realm of dreams and fantasy; give it just as much attention as the waking, conscious state. The exercises that follow will help you begin to sensitize yourself for working with your unconscious imagination.

Sit comfortably and close your eyes. Picture yourself at an inspiring place in nature—perhaps in the forest, on a beach, or on top of a magestic mountain. You might want to remember a personal experience or create something completely new. Some people can form vivid pictures whereas others have only a vague generalized sense: The vividness of imagery varies from person to person. Whatever your natural tendency for visualization, work with it as it is.

Let your imagination roam around the area, but do not present yourself with a plan or goal. Simply be curious and meander about, or imaginatively sit down to experience more fully. When you feel that you have explored enough, open your eyes.

Often dreams help to balance out deficits in our everyday life, providing yin where there is too much yang, or vice versa. We can learn about deeper aspects of ourselves, solve problems unconsciously, or even come up with creative ideas from dreams. You can encourage the process by having a positive, open curiosity about your dreams.

Remembering Dreams

The first step is to remember your dreams. Some people recall dreams readily, others have more difficulty. If you do not recall your dreams, you can try to improve your memory of them. Just before you go to sleep each night, remind yourself that you are interested in remembering your dreams. When you wake up the next morning, shift awake slowly. Do not open your eyes immediately. Lay back, relax, and let yourself recapture bits of the dream. Have a pencil and paper near your bed and jot down notes. Some people may prefer to use a tape recorder.

Accepting Dreams

You will have a better chance of remembering your dreams if you accept what your inner mind offers. Do not pass judgment on your dreams, nor should you try to impose a narrow symbolic interpretation. Interpretive dream work has its place for an analytical understanding, but it leads you away from Tao. For a Taoist approach, the process is more spontaneous.

Review the dream. Notice what you feel as you think about it again. Let meanings occur to you spontaneously. Just as the Yellow Emperor was able to find meaningful understandings in his journey dream (see Chapter 4), you will begin to make discoveries from your dreams. If nothing occurs to you, accept that for now, but be open for any insights that might occur to you at another time. Do not contend with the dream or with your concerns about the dream, include both. The dream is a path to deeper understanding.

Working with Dreams

Taoist sages often guided people to new understandings through the use of dreams and daydreams. This exercise can open the doorway for you to do this yourself.

Think of a situation that bothers you, perhaps a problem in the workplace, maybe a difficulty at home. Sit comfortably and close your eyes. Imagine a typical interaction in this situation. Visualize yourself there, doing what you normally do. Next, imagine the same situation as if all the problems were gone. Visualize yourself there. How do you behave now? Compare the two situations, back and forth. What is different? What is similar? Do you begin to get ideas about what you can do to change things?

Conclusion

Taoism can guide you back to your center. When you attune yourself to Tao, you gain sensitivity, flexibility, a sixth sense for the best course to follow. You are energized by the flow of chi, allowing it to circulate freely and nourish you day by day. You evolve from the Tao, poised between yin and yang, following the natural flow of your life as it unfolds.

With Tao as your inspiration and chi as your vitality, you can allow yourself to develop fully and become all that you hope to be. Find your balance in motion as you travel the Path, enjoying the Way!

Timeline

SHANG DYNASTY
1500 B.C.E.–1027 B.C.E.

Legendary Yellow Emperor Dates unknown
•
I Ching
1150 B.C.E. exact dates unknown authorship attributed to
King Wen or Yellow Emperor

....

CHOU DYNASTY
1027 B.C.E.– 221 B.C.E.
•
Lao-tzu
b. 604 B.C.E.
•
Confucius b. 551 B.C.E.
•
Chuang-tzu 369 – 286 B.C.E.
•
Lieh-tzu Approximately 400 – 200 B.C.E.;
exact dates unknown
•
Yang Chu dates unknown

•

Mencius 372 – 289 B.C.E.

....

CH 'IN DYNASTY
221 B.C.E.– 207 B.C.E.

•

Great Wall of China built

....

HAN DYNASTY
200 B.C.E.– C.E. 221

•

Ssu-ma Tan
d. 110 B.C.E. Historian

•

Ssu-ma Ch'ien 145 – 86 B.C.E.
Son of Tan, Historian

•

Yu Chi Approximately 150
Author of *The Way of Grand* Peace and founder of the Way of
Grand Peace Sect

•

Chang Ling Founder of Heavenly Masters Sect
b. between 157–178

•

Yellow Turban Rebellion begins C.E. 184

•

Chang Lu 188–220
Grandson Chang Ling Heavenly Masters Sect

•

Dragon-Tiger Classic
C.E. 220 Early Alchemy Text

. . . .

ERA OF DIVISION
221 B.C.E.– C.E. 589

•

Neo-Taoists 220 – C.E. 420

•

Liu Ling
221–300 Neo-Taoists

•

Wang Hui-chih
d. 388 Neo-Taoists

•

Wang Pi
226–249 Neo-Taoists

•

Ku-Kai 344–406
Chinese Painter

•

Tsung Ping 373–443
Chinese Painter

•

Wang Wei 415–443
Chinese Painter

•

Six Canons
500
Author Hsieh-Ho Taoist Painting Manual

....

T'ANG DYNASTY
618–906

•

Water-Dragon Classic
600
First manual of Feng Shui

•

Ancester Lu b. 646
Founder of The School of Complete Reality

•

Shapes and Forms School of Feng Shui 850
founded by Yang Yung Sung

....

SUNG DYNASTY
960–1279

•

Compass School of Feng Shui founded 1050

•

Fukien School of Feng Shui founded 1100

....

MONGOL RULE
1279–1368

•

Cheng San-feng 1300
Founder of Tai Chi Chuan

....

MING DYNASTY
1368–1644

....

CH 'ING DYNASTY
1644–1911

•

Yang Lu Ch'an 1799–1872
Founder of Yang style Tai Chi Chuan

•

Wu Yu-hsiung 1812–1880
Founder of Wu style Tai Chi Chuan

Taoism, Tai Chi and Mindfulness Resources

Tai Chi and Mindfulness Apps

These apps for smartphones and tablets (iOS and Android versions) are helpful for supporting one's daily tai chi, mindfulness and meditation practice and connecting with worldwide practice communities. Enjoy!

Master Yang opens the world of long-form Yang-style tai chi, offering step-by-step instructions, including front and rear views, as well as an eye-opening tutorial on the detailed theories informing the practice (https://apps.apple.com/us/app/id904366987?mt=8).

For those with a little less time to spare, Master Li's seven-minute Meditate & Move app is just the thing. Recharge or start your day with an energy boost following these easy-to-do moves from Chinese qi gong and traditional tai chi (https://apps.apple.com/us/app/id1048130885?mt=8).

The Insight Timer app supports your meditation with bells for daily practice and allows you to connect with a worldwide meditation community (https://insighttimer.com).

The Lotus Bud Mindfulness Bell offers a simple daytime reminder to mindfully awaken throughout your day (https://apps.apple.com/us/app/lotus-bud-mindfulness-bell/id502329366).

The Headspace app, featured in the *New York Times*, makes practicing simple mindfulness techniques easy (https://www.headspace.com/headspace-meditation-app).

The Mindfulness Bell app allows you to set a bell that rings randomly as a reminder to stop and breathe (https://apps.apple.com/us/app/mindfulness-bell/id380816407?mt=).

Publications

Bays, Chan Chozen. *Mindful Eating: A Guide to Rediscovering A Healthy and Joyful Relationship with Food*. Shambhala Publications, 2009.

Brach, Tara. *Radical Acceptance: Embracing Your Life with the Heart of a Buddha*. New York: Bantam, 2004.

Braza, Jerry. *Moment by Moment: The Art and Practice of Mindfulness*. Vermont: Tuttle Publishing, 1997

Braza, Jerry. *The Seeds of Love: Growing Mindful Relationships*. Vermont: Tuttle Publishing, 2011.

Busch, Charles. *Soft as Water*. Sweden: Irene Publishing, 2018.

Chodron, Pema. *When Things Fall Apart: Heart Advice for Difficult Times*. Shambhala, 2016.

Cope, Stephen. *Soul Friends: The Transforming Power of Deep Human Connection*. Hay House, 2017.

The Dalai Lama and Tutu, Desmond. *The Book of Joy: Lasting Happiness in a Changing World*. Avery, 2016.

Davis, Martha and Robbins, Elizabeth. *The Relaxation and Stress Reduction Workbook*. New Harbinger, 2019.

Delio, Illio. *The Humility of God*. Franciscan Media, 2006.

Gach, Gary. *Pause Breathe Smile.* Boulder: Sounds True, 2018.

Goldstein, Joseph. *Mindfulness: A Practical Guide to Awakening.* Sounds True, 2016.

Goleman, Daniel and Davidson, Richard. *Altered Traits: Science Reveals How Mediation Changes Your Mind, Brain and Body.* Avery, 2018.

Halifax, Joan. *Standing at the Edge.* New York: Flatiron Book, 2018.

Hanh, Thich Nhat. (Series): *How to Sit, How to Love, How to Walk, How to Eat.* Parallax Press, 2014-15.

_____. *Miracle of Mindfulness.* Beacon Press, 1999.

_____. *Living Buddha, Living Christ.* New York: Riverhead Books, 1995.

_____. *Inside the Now.* Berkeley: Parallax Press, 2015.

_____. *True Love.* Boston: Shambhala Publications, 2004

Hanson, Rick. *Hardwiring for Happiness.* New York: Harmony, 2013.

_____. *The Practical Science of the Buddha's Brain.* Oakland: New Harbinger, 2009

Kabat-Zinn, Jon. *Full Catastrophe Living.* Bantam, 2013.

Kahneman, Daniel. *Thinking Fast and Slow.* FSG, 2013.

Karas, Elaine Miller. *Building Resilience to Trauma and Community Resilience Models.* Routledge, 2015.

Kornfield, Jack. *A Path with Heart: A Guide Through the Perils and Promises of Spiritual Life.* New York, Bantam, 1993.

Linehan, Marsha. *Building a Life Worth Living.* Random House, 2020.

Masters, Robert. *Bringing Your Shadow Out of the Dark*. Sounds True, 2018.

Nghiem, Sister Dang. *Mindfulness as Medicine*. Berkeley: Parallax Press, 2015.

O'Donohue, John. *Anam Cara*. Harper Collins, 1998.

————. *To Bless the Space Between Us: A Book of Blessings*. Double Day, 2008.

Ostaseski, Frank. *The Five Invitations: Discovering What Death Can Teach Us About Living Fully*. Flatiron Books, 2019.

Radmacher, Mary Anne. *Lean forward into Your Life*. Conari Press, 2015.

Rohr, Richard. *Falling Upward: A Spirituality for the Two Halves of Life*. Jossey-Bass, 2011.

Salzberg, Sharon. *The Revolutionary Art of Happiness*. Shambhala Publications, 2002.

Schneider, Gary. *Ten Breaths to Happiness. Berkeley: Parallax Press, 2009*

Simpkins, C. Alexander, and Annellen M. Simpkins. 1997. *Zen Around the World*. Boston: Tuttle Publishing.

————. 1999. *Simple Zen: A Guide to Living in Balance*. Boston: Tuttle Publishing.

————. 1996. *Principles of Meditation*. Boston: Tuttle Publishing.

————. 1997. *Living Meditation*. Boston: Tuttle Publishing.

————. 1998. *Meditation from Thought to Action*. Boston: Tuttle Publishing.

Stella, Tom. *Finding God Beyond Religion*. Skylight Paths, 2013.

Suzuki, Shunryu. *Zen Mind, Beginner's Mind*, (50th Anniversary), Shambhala Publications, 2020.

Teasdale, Wayne. *The Mystic Heart*. Novato: New World Library, 2001.

Tolle, Eckhart. *The Power of Now*. Novato: The New World Library, 1999.

Van der kolk, Bessel. *The Body Keeps the Score: Brain, Mind, and Body in the Healing of Trauma*. Penguin Books, 2015.

Williams, Florence. *The Nature Fix: Why Nature Makes Us Happier, Healthier, and More Creative*. New York: Norton, 2018

"Books to Span the East and West"

Tuttle Publishing was founded in 1832 in the small New England town of Rutland, Vermont [USA]. Our core values remain as strong today as they were then—to publish best-in-class books which bring people together one page at a time. In 1948, we established a publishing outpost in Japan—and Tuttle is now a leader in publishing English-language books about the arts, languages and cultures of Asia. The world has become a much smaller place today and Asia's economic and cultural influence has grown. Yet the need for meaningful dialogue and information about this diverse region has never been greater. Over the past seven decades, Tuttle has published thousands of books on subjects ranging from martial arts and paper crafts to language learning and literature—and our talented authors, illustrators, designers and photographers have won many prestigious awards. We welcome you to explore the wealth of information available on Asia at www.tuttlepublishing.com.

Published by Tuttle Publishing, an imprint of Periplus Editions (HK) Ltd.
www.tuttlepublishing.com

Copyright © 2020 C. Alexander Simpkins

Library of Congress Cataloging-in-Publication Data in process

Hardcover ISBN: 978-0-8048-5268-5

Ebook ISBN: 978-1-4629-2213-0

29 28 27 26 25
10 9 8 7 6 5 4 3   2502CM

Printed in China

TUTTLE PUBLISHING® is a registered trademark of Tuttle Publishing, a division of Periplus Editions (HK) Ltd.

Distributed by

North America, Latin America & Europe
Tuttle Publishing
364 Innovation Drive
North Clarendon
VT 05759-9436 U.S.A.
Tel: 1 (802) 773-8930
Fax: 1 (802) 773-6993
info@tuttlepublishing.com
www.tuttlepublishing.com

Japan
Tuttle Publishing
Yaekari Building 3rd Floor
5-4-12 Osaki Shinagawa-ku
Tokyo 1410032, Japan
Tel: (81) 3 5437 0171
Fax: (81) 3 5437 0755
sales@tuttle.co.jp
www.tuttle.co.jp

Asia Pacific
Berkeley Books Pte. Ltd.
3 Kallang Sector, #04-01
Singapore 349278
Tel: (65) 67412178
Fax: (65) 67412179
inquiries@periplus.com.sg
www.tuttlepublishing.com